Seeing Fractions
A Unit for the Upper Elementary Grades

Developed by
TERC (Technical Education Research Centers, Inc.)
for the California Department of Education

Written by Rebecca B. Corwin,
Susan Jo Russell, and Cornelia C. Tierney

Credits

STAFF

CURRICULUM

Rebecca B. Corwin
Susan Jo Russell
Cornelia C. Tierney

RESEARCH AND EVALUATION

Janice R. Mokros
Mark Ogonowski
Alana Parkes
Judy Storeygard
Amy Shulman Weinberg

DESIGN AND PRODUCTION

John Abbe
Edith Alvarenga
LeAnn Davis
Elisabeth Roberts

COOPERATING TEACHERS

Nancy Cangiano
Kathy Cline
Jorge de la O
Diane Doe
Joan Easterday
Barbara Fox
Diane Garfield
Zelda Gold
Francine Hiller
Caren Holtzman

Elisabeth Javor
Deborah Kitchens
Sandra Lam
Belinda Lister
Bruce MacDonald
Suzanne McGrath
Lynette Meyer
Mary Patton
Jean Pettit
Janice Roche

Suzy Ronfeldt
Elaine Rosenfield
Patti Russo
Nancy Shepherd
Leslie Stirnus
Jay Sugarman
Elizabeth Sullivan
Jim Swaim
Traci Wierman

Seeing Fractions was developed by Rebecca B. Corwin, Susan Jo Russell, and Cornelia C. Tierney at the Technical Education Research Centers, Inc., under contract to the California Department of Education, Joan Akers, Mathematics Education Consultant—Liaison. The document was published by the Department, 721 Capitol Mall, Sacramento, California (mailing address: P.O. Box 944272, Sacramento, CA 94244-2720).

Copies of this publication are available for $7 each, plus sales tax for California residents, from the Bureau of Publications, Sales Unit, California Department of Education, P.O. Box 271, Sacramento, CA 95812-0271.

A list of other publications available from the Department can be found at the back of this publication.

ISBN 0-8011-0926-4

CONTENTS

How this unit was developed

This unit was trial tested in about 30 classrooms, grades 4 through 6. The classrooms were diverse, including children from many socioeconomic and ethnic groups, as well as students with identified special needs and students for whom English is a second language.

Based on classroom observation and teacher feedback from two rounds of trials, the unit was extensively revised. Teacher Notes and Dialogue Boxes were developed to address issues raised by these classroom experiences.

While the authors accept all responsibility for what finally appears in this book, we are indebted to many other educators and researchers who have investigated student understanding of fractions. In particular, we are grateful for the efforts of the participating teachers, whose invaluable observations and advice consistently pushed us to rethink our ideas and approaches, and for feedback and comments from Joan Akers, Marilyn Burns, and Mark Ogonowski.

All of the activities in this unit are related to approaches which have been used by many other educators and have appeared in many different forms. While it is impossible to acknowledge all of those who have worked with these models previously, we were particularly influenced by the work of the Nuffield Mathematics Project in England; "How to teach fractions so as to be useful" by the Research group on Mathematics Education of the State University of Utrecht, The Netherlands; the Educational Technology Center Fractions Project at Harvard University; and the teacher's manual for the Scott, Foresman, & Co. fifth grade mathematics textbook from the early 1960s.

Introduction

I. AN OVERVIEW OF FRACTIONS

Seeing Fractions is designed to help students become aware of the variety
of ways in which fractions are commonly used, develop a repertoire of
visual models for fractions, and apply these models flexibly and
appropriately as they solve problems with fractions. Fractional notation is
used in many different ways, depending on what context it is used to
describe. Fractions may express, for example, part of the area of a shape
(two of six parts of the square), part of a group of things (there were 23
dogs out of the total of 100 pets), part of a length (a third of the distance
from here to there), or a rate (four cents for ten gumballs). In solving
problems with fractions, many powerful mathematics users call on
internalized images or models that allow them to visualize fractions. These
images often provide the basis for estimating, finding equivalents,
comparing, and carrying out operations with fractions. When a student can
visualize 4/9 as a little less than a half, she has the tools to estimate 4/9
of 16 and to evaluate the results of her exact computation, if it is needed,
with reference to her estimate ("a little less than 8, probably about 7").

This teaching unit presents fraction activities in four contexts. In the first
module, students explore basic part-whole concepts, find some equivalent
fractions, and gain knowledge about relative size and relationships of
fractions while working in a geometric context with an area model of
fractions. The second module focuses on problems with rates as a context
for exploring number patterns and comparing fractions. In the third
module, students again work with a part-whole model doing cookie sharing
to develop notions of equivalence and addition of fractions. They also
investigate ways of showing parts of a group. The fourth module centers on
a linear measurement model of fractions, and students create their own
representations of fractions of a unit. In the last module, students collect
and analyze data; they use fractions to compare the data from their own
class with the results from other classes.

WHAT'S SO HARD ABOUT FRACTIONS?

Fractions are complicated. In order to interpret and use fractions, the
student must consider relationships— either between parts and wholes or
between different quantities. When a student sees 2/3, he or she must
think about the 2 and the 3 separately as well as how the two numbers are
related. Familiar computational routines seem not to work any more;
students encounter a problem like 7/15 divided by 2/3 and are told that
the way to solve it is to multiply. This is distinctly confusing.

Connecting fraction operations to daily life can be difficult for teachers.
Finding practical models for fractions is difficult, and the curriculum often
emphasizes only the traditional pie model or the "part-of-a-group" model.
The students are given these models as illustrations but do not participate
in constructing and exploring them.

Commonsense fractions (halves, fourths) are easy for students to visualize and generally easy for them to operate with. For example, students often know how big a half is and can also show two-thirds of a unit. However, when symbols are introduced, the students are tempted to move to rapid numeral manipulation, following rote procedures to get correct answers. So when faced with computation problems which use the same fractions they are able to visualize, like 1/2 and 2/3, they appear to lose their commonsense knowledge and manipulate those symbols blindly. In another context, they may "know" that a half and two-thirds must be a little over one complete unit, but they still might add 1/2 and 2/3 on paper and get 3/5. Even students who are able to use correct procedures to complete a practice page in the workbook may still not have an understanding of the underlying ideas that should guide their work in using fractions to solve real problems.

FRACTIONS IN THE INTERMEDIATE GRADES

Fractions and fraction operations can be a frustrating part of the curriculum for many students. Although students have typically learned to use the algorithms for finding equivalent fractions and for addition and subtraction of fractions, they often have no real grasp of many of the "big ideas" about fractions, ideas which are the foundation of the symbolic manipulation typical of the upper grade curriculum. The following critical ideas lead to students' constructing and using models of fractions for reasoning about new situations.

❑ A fraction can be used to describe all kinds of situations, including parts of one thing, parts of a group of things, and rates.

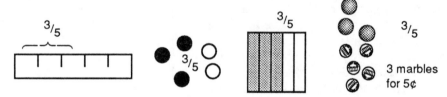

❑ Different fractions can express the same relationships. Half of a cake is the same amount as two fourths of the same cake. Three marbles for 5¢ (3/5) and six marbles for 10¢ (6/10) are instances of the same rate of marbles and money.

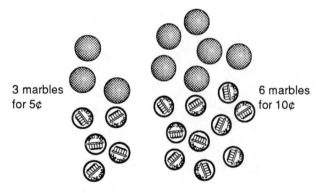

3 marbles
for 5¢

6 marbles
for 10¢

❑ Estimation of the size of a fraction or the results of an operation with fractions is vital to understanding fractions. A good sense of the relative size of familiar fractions allows students to compare unfamiliar fractions with familiar ones and to estimate the results of fraction operations with some confidence:

19 out of 31 students take the bus to school—19/31—that's about 2/3 of the class.

❑ In part-whole situations, equal fractions of a whole are the same size; when dividing something into halves or into fourths, the unit is divided into equal pieces.

However, those pieces need not look the same. These squares are both divided into halves even though, in the second case, the halves are not congruent:

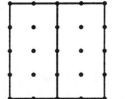 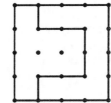

❑ The comparative order of fractions is absolute, but in part-whole situations their size is relative to the size of their units.

1/2 is always bigger than 1/4, but the half in the first picture is smaller than the quarter in the second:

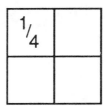

❑ To understand a part-whole model, you have to keep in mind the whole, even when the whole disappears and only the fraction is being used.

This is 2/3 of something. What does the whole look like?

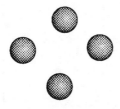

❑ In part-whole situations, fractions which are larger than unit fractions (fractions with 1 in the numerator) are constructed by repeating the unit fraction (e.g., 2/3 is 1/3 and 1/3).

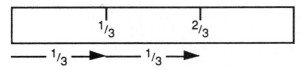

❏ When fractions are used to express rates, the same rate describes a series of ratios. If two apples cost 25¢, the rate 2 apples for 25¢ (2/25) applies to a purchase of 4 apples (4/50), 6 apples (6/75), and so forth.

SLOWING DOWN

Moving slowly through these modules is worth the effort. Taking the time to work at understanding the topic of fractions will only help all students. The "memorizers" have another chance to learn the deep concepts; so do the students who have not yet been able to make connections from their own models of fractions to the algorithms. Teachers who use this unit have found that many of their quicker students have enjoyed the opportunity to slow down and to investigate and explore concepts that were given short shrift previously.

The students who have had difficulty learning procedures may excel at visual estimation and pattern finding. Those who most readily learn procedures and who manipulate symbols happily may find that they need to rethink their explanations of operations and to extend their understanding to incorporate more flexible and comprehensive reasoning.

Moving the emphasis from getting the correct answer to explaining and justifying solution strategies helps all students. Those who work quickly with the symbols are required to make sense of those manipulations; those who work slowly with materials are required to explain their thinking. Every student can find moments when he or she is the one in the group who can build a good model or think through a problem or find a number pattern. When the process matters more than the answer, students find many ways of sharing their methods and comparing their results. They have the opportunity to construct a new reality.

WHAT WILL STUDENTS LEARN ABOUT FRACTIONS?

Mastery of algorithms is not the goal of this unit. Rather, the emphasis is on learning to think about fractions in ways that make sense to the individual child who is thinking about them. Students cannot be expected to understand completely something presented to them in a relatively brief time span. They need to come back to these ideas and these topics frequently over time. Ideas that were incompletely learned in earlier grades are reconsidered, and time is taken to revisit those concepts. Students can and will deepen their understanding of many ideas as they work on this unit, but we cannot assume that students can immediately build on newly grasped concepts. If you expect that your students will need to revisit many of these ideas over time, you will help everyone to see mathematics as a process of development rather than as a set of hurdles to be jumped once and only once.

How do we know they know? When the answer to the problem is the goal of teaching, assessment and evaluation are easy. Students can be tested to see whether they can find correct answers. Further, their computational speed can be measured. Those who work slowly or those who are inaccurate are penalized equally. When the reasoning behind the choices and the way of reaching a solution are the focus of the classroom, assessment becomes a more complex issue.

How can we tell a child "knows" about thirds or fourths? Observing that student at work can go a long way toward letting us know how she is thinking. Finding an interesting problem for students to work on, listening to their conversations, and observing their methods tells a great deal. Sitting down with an individual student to ask questions that probe her understanding also adds to your understanding of that child's thinking, as does reading her written work.

In order to do informal assessment of students' mathematical understanding, combinations of observation, written work, and one-to-one interviews will tell the most. Keeping students' written mathematics work in portfolios (as writing teachers routinely keep students' written work) will provide a record of their progress during the year. Talking with individuals to understand better their thinking about fractions will clarify your understanding. Sitting with groups as they work on problems may tell you even more.

At the end of each module we provide suggestions for assessment. Some of these are problems designed for assessing students' understanding, but others are ways to use the activities in the module as assessment as well as instruction. We suggest you read these suggestions before you begin each module.

II. TEACHING FOR UNDERSTANDING

The National Council of Teachers of Mathematics, in its Curriculum and Evaluation Standards for School Mathematics (1989), recommends that the mathematics curriculum be changed to meet today's economic and social needs. They see major goals for students as:

❑ learning to value mathematics

❑ becoming confident in one's own ability

❑ becoming a mathematical problem solver

❑ learning to communicate mathematically

❑ learning to reason mathematically.

California, as well, has challenged teachers to think about these new emphases for mathematics teaching and learning. A new framework for the teaching of mathematics, K–12 that is being written suggests that mathematics teaching can be changed to take into better account our knowledge about children's development as learners. Further, better supports and tools can be provided to help all of our students to understand and make sense of mathematics. Among the most important aspects of this conception of mathematics teaching and learning are the following:

CONSTRUCTING MATHEMATICAL MODELS

Abstract reasoning is based on internalized models of our own actions. Students must construct their own mathematical models in order to have real power over key mathematical ideas. Simply being presented with a model someone else has found useful does not give students this power. In using fractions, for example, students need to cut up units, to divide wholes, and to compare parts. Whether students develop an area model, a linear model, a discrete model, or another model of a fraction, it will serve as a tool for understanding when it can be used and referred to often, compared with models constructed by others, and used as the basis of beginning computational experiences.

Typically students are asked to interpret others' models of fractions. In this unit they construct their own models and compare them with their peers'. For example, in many school lessons, students have been asked to shade in the pre-drawn parts of a whole:

 Color in 2/3

Most students are able to color two out of three pieces, and they appear to understand the fraction concept. However, when these same students are asked to construct their own picture of 2/3, we often see them create pictures with unequal pieces:

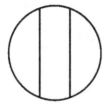

Only by constructing their own models and working in a variety of different contexts do students develop the idea for themselves that all the pieces must be equal in order to have created two-thirds of a pizza or a cookie. And, as students construct their own models, we gain much more insight into their understanding.

TEACHING IS NOT TELLING

When the goals of the curriculum are more important than students' methods of reaching those goals, we often end up pushing students too hard. We tell them what to do, we encourage shortcuts that are adult constructs, and we rush students to use the formal algorithms that embody those shortcuts. This kind of teaching is exhausting for all concerned; and although students may memorize routines and procedures for doing problems, they are unlikely to have the time to contemplate and compare methods, to talk about their work, and to reason through their own processes. This loss of understanding creates a weak foundation for reasoning in current and later mathematics work and destroys students' faith in their own powers of invention. Rather than help them trust their intelligence and thoughtfulness, telling students how to do problems has the long-term effect of disempowering them mathematically.

The emphasis in talking about fractions is often on listening to the teacher's explanation. We explain a solution method to the class, students try it, and the correct answer is set up as a model. When students explain their methods to each other, they often rely on telling alone. In this unit, emphasis is placed on visual methods and on explanations given by students, so that all students have the opportunity to build their own models and work with their own methods. Learning can go on even when the teacher is not part of the discussion!

Discussions in which students compare their methods and talk about processes require time. Teachers find that their roles must change from question-answerer to question-asker. Finding ways of asking questions that help classes compare their methods as well as their results is not always easy. Many teachers find that focusing on method rather than on answers and correctness helps their students feel more open when talking about their own approaches. Questions such as, "How were you thinking about it?" "What did you decide to do about the extra pieces?" "Did everyone in your group have the same method?" "Who else used a method like Sarah's?" will help. If you can keep an open mind about methods you think are tedious, complicated, or misguided, you will find your students more and more eager to examine and improve their methods.

COMMUNICATING ABOUT MATHEMATICAL IDEAS

Mathematicians talk and write and build models about their ideas. At the heart of mathematics is the idea of communication. We all want a generation of mathematics students who can build and model their ideas and tell others about them. Just as your students need to discuss and clarify their ideas, they need to find ways of communicating their ideas and their methods to others. Writing, talking, drawing, modelling— all are ways of communicating. In this unit we include places to write or draw or talk; you may want to find more places for your students to communicate their ideas. Bulletin board displays, stories in the school newspaper, notes home to parents, ideas for younger students, writing mathematics books— all can be ways for your class to explain, clarify, and extend their own communication skills in mathematics.

Gradually, as students mature in their thinking and their experience, they will adopt more and more of the conventional expressions used in formal mathematics. Those conventions will make sense to them, and they will use them more skillfully as they see reasons for communicating ideas in mathematics.

THE ROLE OF FRUSTRATION IN LEARNING MATHEMATICS

Although many students believe that they should "get it" right away in mathematics, that is not the case. Adult mathematicians spend much of their time talking with colleagues or trying again and again to find a way in to a special problem. Approaches to mathematical problems are tried, explored, rejected, talked about, compared, and changed. The same should be true of our students— they need to try things, to come up against walls, and to try in a different way. Without the knowledge that mathematics is one part inspiration and fifty parts hard work, they believe that they are incompetent if they do not understand a problem instantly.

It is hard to allow our students to struggle with their frustration. Many of them believe that the only reasonable school endeavors are tiny bite-sized pieces that can be swallowed with no effort. Until recently most school tasks were cut up into smaller and smaller pieces until students could walk through many complicated ideas without realizing that they were learning something important. Because of that, your students may resist trying their own methods and tolerating their own confusion, frustration, and uncertainty. As they proceed through these sessions, however, you will see them learn to try their own ideas and to experience frustration as a natural part of learning something important.

Your role is still vital in your students' learning, even if you are not telling them what to do or breaking down the task for them. Asking the right question, reassuring them that learning takes time, engaging with them in their investigations are all important aspects of a new role in teaching mathematics. Helping your students make sense of their own methods, helping them express their confusion, and helping them learn from each other's approaches will give them much more than telling them will do.

III. TEACHING THIS UNIT

As you begin to plan and teach this unit, there are some aspects of its approach you may want to think about.

MANIPULATIVES

Each of the five modules in the unit is based on students' use of some concrete materials to model fractional relationships. It is essential that you use the manipulative materials even though your students may seem "beyond" manipulatives. Experience has repeatedly shown that as problems become challenging and complex, the students who can use materials to build models to think with are in a much better situation than those who merely use the numbers.

Your attitude toward materials will make a difference. Some teachers pass out materials as a matter of course, encourage their students to use materials, and make the choice inviting and rewarding. Others leave materials on the side of the room and announce that anyone who needs them can get them when they are having a difficult time. It's no wonder that in the second type of classroom most students feel a bit embarrassed to get up and take materials to their seats.

If you solve these problems and work with these materials yourself, you will see how much can be learned from them. There are no natural progressions away from concrete modelling; many adult mathematicians use concrete models as a quite natural way of working with ideas.

You may find additional materials that will enhance your students' learning about fractions. Cuisenaire rods, interconnecting cubes, or pattern blocks can all be used to model fractional relationships.

GROUPING

Many of the activities in this unit require small-group work. Setting up effective small learning groups is an important task. Teachers whose students are used to working in small groups find their students excited and involved, talking eagerly about their methods and encouraging other members of the group to share and compare. Teachers who have done less with cooperative learning in the classroom find that they need to take some extra time at the start of the unit to work with students on their roles in small groups and on their performance in a learning group.

Teachers find that these activities work best with students in pairs. When comparative methods are shared, one pair can turn to another; and those four students can compare their strategies and methods. Groups of three are a top limit for most of these activities, unless your class is very experienced with cooperative learning. You may want to assign students to set groups for each module; you may want to have them stay in their working groups throughout the unit. The criteria you use for establishing groups may depend on students' previous history in small groups; usually a complex mix of factors determines the effectiveness of a working team, and you may have to experiment to find the best balance for your class.

SEQUENCE AND TIMING OF LESSONS

These sessions are planned as a kind of spine to your teaching about fractions. Just as a biological spine gives support, direction, and strength to a body, these lessons are designed as a teaching core. However, a spine is flexible and gains strength through its flexibility. So, too, with these sessions. You may find that you have some ideas about different pacing or different routes through the sessions. Depending on your teaching style and teaching preferences, you may want to extend some sessions and contract others. Some sections and some images may work better for you than others. The intent of this unit is to support your teaching, not to dictate a recipe to you. Your own choices will be important as you teach the unit. Be careful, though, not to limit your teaching choices to those things you think work best only for you! There will be students in your class who learn very differently and who respond to different approaches. It is important to provide experience with a model which is not one of your favorites, because it might just be the key for some of your students.

You may find that your class responds best to some intensive work on one module with time in-between to do other activities. You may want to do the geometry module and then spend some time doing related activities on the geoboard, or with related computer software. You may want to enhance the modules by adding more writing work and by asking your students to deepen their understanding by keeping mathematics journals. Some of the modules may lead directly to topics you want to cover in other subject areas of the curriculum. Again, the choices are yours to make.

TEACHER'S ROLE

A teacher's role in such an active classroom becomes very complex. You will be a provisioner, providing your students suggestions about ideas and materials to explore. You will be a guide, pointing out landmarks in the curriculum as you move along and integrating your students' understanding with other areas of the curriculum. You will function as a question-poser and a problem-presenter, asking the next question to help students explore their understanding. You may also be a learner. Don't be surprised if at times you yourself are also actively involved in constructing new mathematical knowledge of your own!

The California framework encourages teachers to help students develop their thinking and understanding through direct, personal experiences which deepen and broaden their understandings over time. Students will extract different meanings from the same experience, and in small group work they can compare and contrast their understandings with their peers. Over time they can experience some of the confusion and frustration that are part of the process of learning.

Teachers can help students develop persistence in problem solving only through letting them reflect on their ideas with others, and, as they clarify these ideas, learn to question their own thinking. By developing ways of communicating about mathematics and through developing a meaningful language of mathematics, our students learn to make sense of mathematical concepts. We want to empower our students to think productively about complex ideas; we want them to feel good about their own abilities to solve problems.

A chief piece of the role of the teacher is to understand children's understanding of the topic. You will find yourself spending time trying to understand students' thinking, and may well find yourself puzzling out the logic underlying your students' errors. You are a researcher in your classroom, trying to find the meaning in your students' misconceptions and trying to follow their reasoning. Listening is one of the central skills of a classroom researcher. If you listen and jot down some notes, you can ponder about your students' reasoning later. Remember that students are always trying to make sense of what they do.

COMMUNICATING WITH PARENTS

Parents are naturally interested in their children's schoolwork. Parents' expectations about a unit on fractions will be based on their own school experiences, so they may have many questions about what you are doing.

You may want to let parents know that their children are involved in an exciting new unit on fractions that is designed to provide multiple models of fractions. If you stress the in-depth and constructive aspects of this unit, parents are likely to enjoy working with their children at home, giving themselves a chance to relearn these concepts.

During the study of this unit, students are learning many of the same topics their parents learned in school, even though the methods may be different. Those topics include:

- ❑ constructing and naming fractional parts of a whole

- ❑ comparing relative sizes of fractions

- ❑ building, working with, and exploring many different models of fractions

- ❑ comparing fractions to find the best buy

- ❑ finding equivalent fractions using a variety of models

- ❑ calculating the results of addition of fractions

- ❑ exploring number patterns in fractions

- ❑ using fractions to discuss results of data collection.

Students need to work with concrete manipulative models of fractions in order to make sense of fractions and fraction operations. Using their own invented methods, in the unit students begin to compare fractions, find equivalents, and add both fractions and mixed numbers. Because of this need for taking time to work with materials and to construct their own models, it is important that you not assign pages of problems for practice or homework. For the duration of this unit, students must immerse themselves in these models. Their abilities to visualize and to estimate grow and develop as they work with these activities. Purely symbolic work interferes with that development.

HOMEWORK

You may find that you want to assign homework during the duration of this unit. We suggest that you extend the in-school activities so that the children's families can enjoy these models and activities as well. It is likely that some questions will be raised about the work being "too easy" for fifth graders. Didn't they already learn about halves and fourths? These problems present a range of possibilities. Children work on different problems which they set themselves within the same activity, and experienced students have set harder problems for themselves, challenging their own knowledge. There is no question that the fifth graders who have been involved with the development and testing of this unit have needed these activities, have welcomed them, and have learned from them.

You may want to develop some activities that can be done at home and shared in school with peers. For example, the data analysis activities (Module 5) lend themselves to connections with home. Students can expand their data collection to family or neighborhood. Did the grownups at home have pets when they were children? How many? What kind? How old were they when they first got a pet? After these data are collected and recorded, many fractions can be found: the fraction of grownups who never had a pet, the fraction who have cats compared to fractions who have other pets, the fraction who first got pets when they were ten— or whatever patterns the class chooses to explore after data collection.

Perhaps your students would like to explore best buys with their families (Module 4). You may be able to enlist the help of several parents in finding price rates for some particularly interesting item at their neighborhood store. Another possibility is to look for fraction problems at home. Parents do divide things into fractions— pizza, cakes and pies, pans of brownies, quarts of milk. If you can alert your students' parents to what the class is

doing, you may find that they can help find good real-life problems to
share.

Keep alert to problems as they arise in your own environment as well and
you will easily help students make connections between fraction work in
school and the world they live in.

IV. HOW THIS UNIT IS ORGANIZED

This unit includes 5 modules, each of which focuses on a different context
for exploring fractions. Each module requires between 5 and 7 class
sessions, although many of the investigations can be extended beyond the
initial core of work.

Each module includes:

An overview of the module. This overview summarizes what happens in
the classroom, what you will need to prepare ahead of time, and what
important mathematical ideas are emphasized.

Plans for each class session. Although we have attempted to break up
each module into manageable class sessions, we expect that you will often
have to adjust these sessions to fit your class's schedule and pace.
Because teachers have found it helpful, we sometimes include samples of
"teacher talk" in boldface type within session activities. These samples are,
in all cases, intended to be guidelines, not scripts. Modify them to fit your
own style and approach.

Teacher Notes. These notes highlight some of the mathematical ideas
which students work on during each module. They draw on the authors'
observations of students' strategies, approaches, difficulties, and
confusions as they investigate fractions. We suggest that you read all the
Teacher Notes at the end of a session before you start the activities with
your class.

Dialogue Boxes. Discussion is a key component of student thinking and
learning in mathematics. The Dialogue Boxes, based on classroom
episodes, give examples of conversations in which students attempt to
express their understanding of key mathematical ideas.

Module 1: Geometry with fractions

MODULE OVERVIEW

WHAT HAPPENS

The activities in this module focus on developing visual, geometric representations of common fractions and building students' knowledge of common equivalents such as 1/4 and 2/8. In the first three sessions, students use dot paper (provided) or geoboards to construct different ways of representing halves, fourths, and eighths on a 4 x 4 square grid. Then, in the fourth session, they explore ways of combining halves, fourths, eighths, and, if you wish, sixteenths in the same design to construct a whole (see the figures 1.16 and 1.17). In the next two sessions, students follow a similar sequence, using thirds, sixths, and twelfths. They may want to find combinations of these parts which make a whole as well.

Beginning with this module, students are encouraged to keep a folder or notebook of writing and illustrations of their work in this unit. The work they do in geometry will be useful as a reference in other sections of the unit.

Teachers who used this unit found that, even though the geometry activities appear straightforward, their students needed to proceed slowly through this module. Most classes spend one entire session on halves; many spend two. Fourths and eighths also required time for students to think, draw, and discuss their strategies. Often, two more sessions were required for fourths and eighths. Teachers and students invented many extensions for the geometry work which, if the class chose to pursue them, added additional sessions to the module. Some of these extensions are suggested here, and your students may invent others. For all of these reasons, we can only suggest how to spread these activities across a certain number of sessions. We have divided the activities into six sessions of about 45 minutes each. But feel free to alter this division to fit the pace of your class.

WHAT TO PLAN AHEAD OF TIME

❑ On the chalkboard, chart paper, or overhead, draw a few dot patterns, such as those on the provided dot paper (Worksheet 1.1), for use with the whole class. These dot patterns are made using 5 rows with 5 dots in each row, resulting in a 4 x 4 grid of small squares (Session 1):

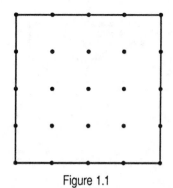

Figure 1.1

❑ Provide enough copies of the 4 x 4 squares (Worksheet 1.1) so that students can experiment freely with halves, fourths, and eighths (about 5–6 copies for each student). If you have geoboards, students can use them instead of paper for experimenting, but they will still need dot paper to record their work. If your students are using geoboards for the first time, provide some additional time for students to explore making shapes with the geoboards before they begin working on halves (Sessions 1–4).

❑ Provide scissors so that students can cut and rearrange, if they wish, to prove that their halves (and other fractions) are equal. Also provide centimeter cubes, if you have them (throughout).

❑ Create several transparencies of Worksheets 1.1 and 1.3 so that students can illustrate their strategies on the overhead (throughout, optional).

❑ Provide copies of Worksheet 1.2, the 6" x 6" square (Sessions 4–6, optional).

❑ Provide enough copies of the 6 x 4 rectangles (Worksheet 1.3) so that students can experiment freely with thirds, sixths, and twelfths. If you have the kind of geoboards which can be put together, students can outline a 6 x 4 rectangle on two side-by-side geoboards (Sessions 5–6).

❑ Provide rulers if you decide to use the large unmarked square (Sessions 4 and 6, optional).

❑ Provide colored pencils, markers, or crayons for students to make final copies of their best designs (throughout, optional).

❑ Provide copies of Worksheet 1.4, the equilateral triangle (optional).

❑ Arrange some way for students to keep their work together, in a folder or notebook.

IMPORTANT MATHEMATICAL IDEAS

Understanding that fractional parts of a whole are equal parts. Even fourth and fifth grade students often do not realize that making halves, thirds, or other fractional divisions of a whole must result in equal parts. Because we often provide diagrams and models which are already divided equally, we do not get a chance to see whether students understand that fractions are equal parts of a whole.

Understanding that equal parts of shapes are not necessarily congruent. In these activities, students encounter situations where the two halves or four quarters of a square do not look the same but are equal in area. Although in many situations the two halves of something are the same shape and size (two halves of a sandwich, for example), halves do not have to be congruent—the same size and shape. A particular half acre of land may be shaped quite differently from some other half acre, but both can still be exactly half of an acre. In many measurement situations, including area, length, and volume, students will find that, for example, one-half or one-fourth of something does not look like another half or fourth of the same quantity.

Visualizing common equivalents. The partitioning of squares into various fractional parts provides models of the relationships of certain common fractions. Students can internalize these images so that they can "see" that one fourth and two eighths are equal or that three eighths is the same as 1 and 1/2 fourths. This model also lays a foundation for addition of common fractions. Students ought to be able to visualize the sum of 1/4 and 2/8 or 1/4 and 3/8 without using an algorithm to find the common denominator and add.

SESSION 1 ACTIVITIES

Introducing halves

Working with the whole class, draw students' attention to the 4 x 4 dot squares on the board. We have found that it helps some students if you connect all the dots around the edge so that students can see the outline of the square clearly. Ask students how they could divide this square in half. Students will probably come up with three common ways:

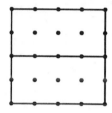 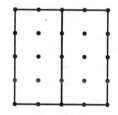 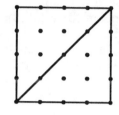

Figure 1.2

Challenge students to come up with other ways to divide the squares in half. At first, students may insist that there are no other ways. Ask them to think about cutting a cookie or a sandwich in half. Could they make the halves fair in some way without making a straight line? Encourage students to illustrate their ideas by sketching them in the air or on the chalkboard.

Tell students that they are going to be working in small groups to find as many ways as they can of dividing the dot squares in half, using straight cuts (as illustrated above) and irregular cuts like these:

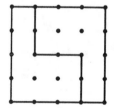 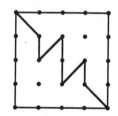 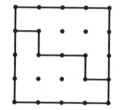

Figure 1.3

If students have not come up with a way to cut the square using a more jagged cut, show them one example. You may need to discuss with them whether or not these are really halves. If this was a brownie, would this be a fair way to cut it in order to give halves to two people?

Small-group work: In how many different ways can you divide a square into halves?

Using copies of the page of 4 x 4 dot squares (Worksheet 1.1), students work in pairs or threes (arrange this in the way you think it will work best in your class) to make as many ways as they can of dividing the square in half. If you have geoboards, students may also work with these to generate different ways of making halves. Working as a group, they generate as many possibilities as they can.

Remember to do connecting activities — 2 (equal parts)

If your students are using geoboards for the first time, give students some time to explore making shapes with the geoboards before they begin working on halves.

Introducing halves which don't look the same

As you circulate among the small groups, notice if groups include possibilities in which the halves do not have the same shapes, such as:

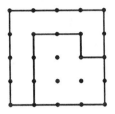 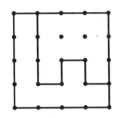 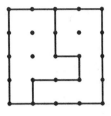

Figure 1.4

Either introduce this idea to each group as you think they are ready, or you may want to have a whole group discussion of this issue. Are the pieces halves if they don't look the same? Would this division be fair if the square were a garden or a brownie? Would the two people get the same amount (of land or brownie)? You may want to make the distinction here between "equal" and "congruent."

Encourage students to develop and articulate their strategies for proving that their halves are equal and provide as many materials as you can to help students develop their own proofs. Some students will count squares. Others may cut one of their halves in pieces and rearrange the pieces on top of the second half to show equality. Centimeter cubes fit on the squares of the dot paper; some students invented methods of using these to help them describe their results.

Sharing strategies and results

When each small group has generated many possibilities, ask students to share some of their favorite ways of making halves. In each case, can the student prove that the division results in two equal pieces? Students enjoy showing their strategies on the chalkboard or overhead.

The pages of halves can be kept in the Fractions Folder or Notebook. Some students may want to make a final page of halves, selecting and coloring their favorites. The halves can also be labeled, as shown:

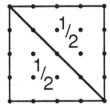 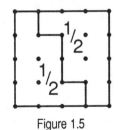 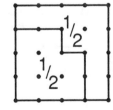

Figure 1.5

SESSIONS 2 AND 3 ACTIVITIES

Introducing fourths and eighths

As students complete their work on halves, have them go on to find fourths of their squares, then eighths. You may want to pause for a whole-group discussion of fourths similar to the discussion of halves in Session 1. Or you may want to start each small group off as they finish their halves.

Again, expect that students will quickly see some of the common ways of dividing a square into fourths (figure 1.6) but will have to think harder about more irregular ways (figure 1.7):

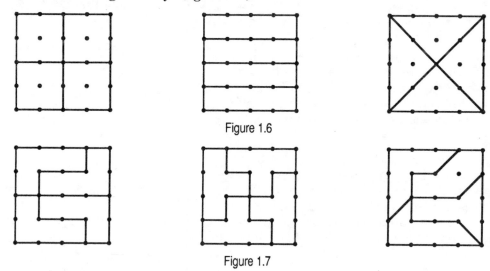

Figure 1.6

Figure 1.7

As students suggest possibilities, ask them to justify how they know that their division has produced fourths in each case. Is it a "fair" division? How do they know for sure?

Small-group work: In how many different ways can you divide a square into fourths and eighths?

Using copies of the page of 4 x 4 dot squares, students generate as many ways as they can of dividing the square into fourths, using the dot paper, or using geoboards first and recording on the dot paper. As you circulate among the small groups, again notice if groups include possibilities in which all of the fourths do not have the same shapes, such as:

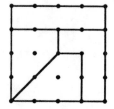 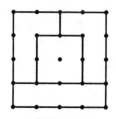 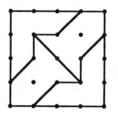

Figure 1.8

Some students may also discover ways of making fourths which are not "attached" but are shown to be one-fourth through use of color and design.

Module 1: Geometry with fractions

For example, in the following design, the two center pieces are each one-fourth, and pairs of opposite corners each make one-fourth:

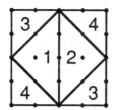

Figure 1.9

The student who made this one argued that even though one corner piece, by itself, is an eighth, he was considering the two corner pieces together. While you can certainly accept a clear student explanation such as this one, keep in mind that pursuing this strategy of "disconnected" fractions can lead to some confusing situations. Once they have discovered this approach, some students become so interested in making patterns that they lose track of the fractions they are trying to construct:

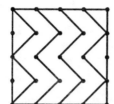

Figure 1.10

When the student who made the square above was asked how it showed fourths, she said, "Well, just combine pieces," but could not explain how to combine them. Later in the module, when students are showing different fractions (e.g., fourths, eighths, and sixteenths) of the same square, other difficulties may arise. For example, in the square below, the eighths are separate pieces, but the fourth is made by combining the two shaded pieces. The relationship between fourths and eighths can no longer be seen very easily:

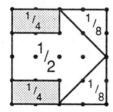

Figure 1.11

One more round: Eighths

When students are finished with fourths, the groups work on eighths, using the same procedures. Again, each student makes a page of eighths for his or her folder:

 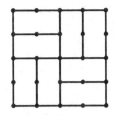 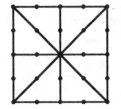

Figure 1.12

NOTE: It isn't necessary for each student to fill a whole page for fourths or eighths. Some students may be more interested than others in finding many possibilities. Some students may work carefully on 5 or 6. Adjust your expectations as seems appropriate to you for each student.

Examples of student work are shown in figures 1.15 and 1.16.

Again, some students may enjoy selecting their favorite fourths and eighths, and coloring and labeling them for their folder.

Discussing and writing justifications for fourths and eighths

At least once during these two sessions, ask students to show examples of their fourths and eighths to the whole class and to explain how they know that the parts are equal. Encourage students to ask each other questions and to share alternative strategies.

At least once during these two sessions, have students write about one of their favorite squares and their strategy for proving that the parts are equal. Writing about mathematics is another way for students to articulate and communicate their ideas (see the TEACHER NOTE: Writing in mathematics). As a way of encouraging writing, one teacher made some homework sheets with two examples of dividing the square invented by students in the class, with a challenge such as, "Prove that Maria's square is divided into fourths. Explain your thinking." Examples of student writing are given in the DIALOGUE BOX: Students write about fractions.

DIALOGUE BOX: STUDENTS WRITE ABOUT FRACTIONS

Here are some examples of student's writing about halves and fourths (in their own words and spellings):

❑ I first drew the fourth and I cut the fourth out and I got them and put them on top of each other and it turned out that they were even. I knew this cause it was congrent. They are diveded into fourths evenly.

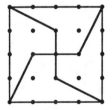

Figure 1.13

❑ I know that this is a half because there are three rectangles in each half but I still had two pieces left over and I found out that each part of the two of the parts I had left over equaled 1/2 of a rectangle, so it's divided into halves.

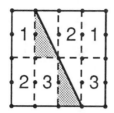

Figure 1.14

❑ I divide things into parts by counting the squares on the geoboard. If I was looking for one-fourth, I'd divide four into sixteen, equals four. Then, I think, there has to be four boxes in each area. Then I fool around with the geoboard and count four boxes in each area so I get my answers. I know I have equal parts by counting the boxes in each area.

❑ I haven't learned much but I've changed my mind about what a half is. A half doesn't have to be symmetrical it just has to be the same size.

TEACHER NOTE: WRITING IN MATHEMATICS

What? Write about mathematics? Typically, students do not write more than numerals in answer boxes in mathematics classes. When would they write about mathematics?

Writing, like talking, is a key way for students to begin to articulate their approaches to problems and their mathematical insights. All too often, a student has the beginnings of an important idea, but drops it. Perhaps it does not occur to her that her idea might be interesting. Perhaps someone else has already found an answer to the problem, so there seems no point in pursuing this new line of thought. By learning to write about the ways they are thinking about a mathematical problem, students gradually learn to record and value their insights. From reading other students' writing, they begin to understand that there are many false starts as well as a variety of successful approaches. And, perhaps most important, by reading student writing, you find out about student ideas which you can pursue further or bring to the attention of other students.

If students have not done writing in mathematics class before, this task will not be a natural one at first. In fact, none of us learned to write about mathematics, so it can be difficult for you to envision what students' writing might be like. Encourage students to write about their solutions to problems and to prove their conclusions, using words and pictures. Ask students to write about discoveries and generalizations which they find as they work. Also urge students to write about approaches which did not work. Discourage writing which veers away from the mathematics towards platitudes which students think you want to hear ("I liked this problem. It was fun").

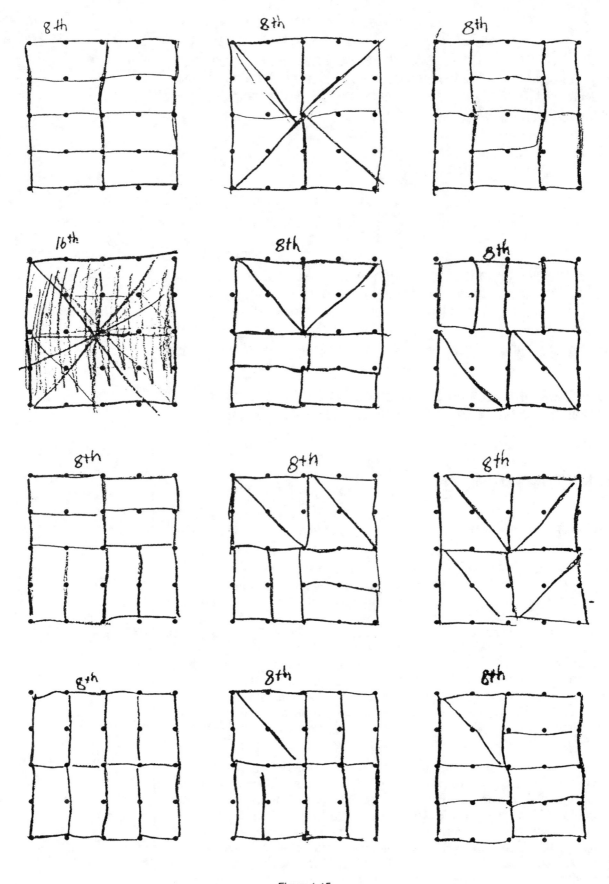

Figure 1.15

Module 1: Geometry with fractions

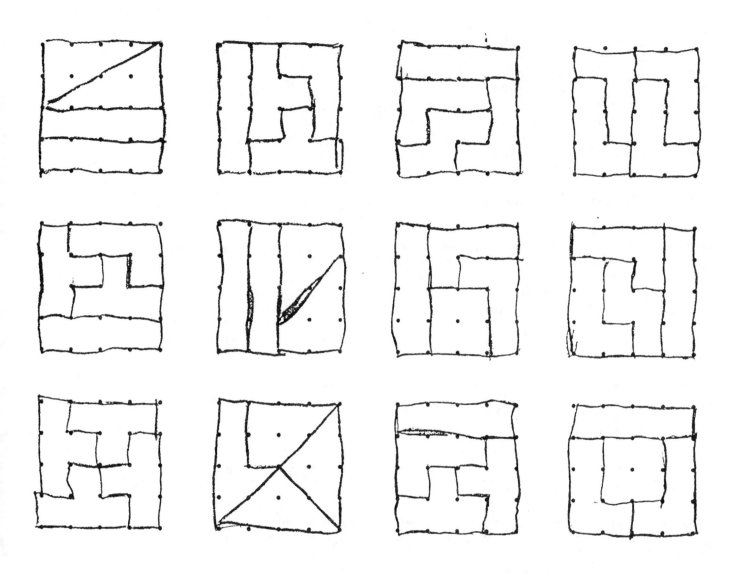

Figure 1.16

SESSION 4 ACTIVITIES

In this session students construct ways of dividing a whole into a combination of halves, fourths, and eighths. Two options for this work— using the dot squares (Worksheet 1.1) and using a large blank square (Worksheet 1.2)— are provided. You may want to have your students do just one of these or both. Students are, of course, quite familiar by now with the dot squares and will be able to apply what they have done in Sessions 1–3 to their work with dot squares. In some ways, Option 1 is more straightforward for you and your students. However, Option 2, work with the large, blank square, provides the opportunity to integrate some measuring activities into this module. While it will initially be more difficult, students do develop a variety of strategies for approaching this task and often come up with designs which are unique, creative, and mathematically interesting.

Option 1: Combining different fractions on the dot squares

Today you're going to make another page for your folder which will show how halves and fourths and eighths are related to each other. When you divided up your dot squares before, you used only halves on some, only fourths on others. But now you're going to figure out how to combine all of them in the same square. For example, on your dot squares, can you think of a way you could have shown halves and fourths on the same square?

Encourage students to come up with a few of their own ideas, which can be displayed on the board. For example, they might think of designs such as these:

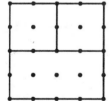 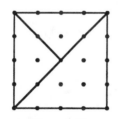 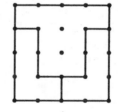

Figure 1.17

Today's challenge is to combine halves, fourths, and eighths all in one design. You can look at your pages of halves, fourths, and eighths to give you ideas about how to do this. This time, label the parts of your design with the fraction for each part, and make sure you can prove what each part is.

Ask students to decide how they would label the examples you have already put on the board.

Students work in their small groups to create combinations of halves, fourths, and eighths. Some students will also want to include sixteenths.

Option 2: Combining different fractions on the blank square

Show students the 6" x 6" square they will be working with (Worksheet 1.2). Don't tell them how long the sides are— they will do their own measuring in their small groups. Then show them the example of a square divided into halves, fourths, and eighths (figure 1.18), and say something like:

Here is one way that one student did this. This is just an idea. There are many different designs which will work to solve this problem. You can use the halves, fourths, and eighths you already did to give you other ideas. The only rule is that you have to include halves, fourths, and eighths in the same square. There are plenty of these squares to work with. You have time to do a few rough drafts to experiment. When you find a design you really like, you can make your final draft, color it, and label all the parts with their fractions.

Small-group work: Making a square of halves, fourths, and eighths

In their small groups, students work on rough drafts of their designs. Although each student makes his or her own design, we encourage students to work in groups to share ideas. It is fine if two students decide to collaborate and each of them makes the same design.

A variety of strategies for dividing up the square may emerge. In order to prove that their parts are halves, fourths, or eighths, some students may fold the square. Others may cut and rearrange pieces from one square on top of another square. Others will measure.

If students are working with the large blank square, there will inevitably be some frustration and confusion as students try to figure out how to divide the square into halves and fourths without the guidance of the dots which they are used to. Acknowledge to students that this task is more difficult and challenging. As you circulate, ask students to find out how big their squares are. How can they find exactly the middle of a side? How do they find half of a half of a side? Encourage students to solve these problems by working together.

Working with the large blank square will give students additional opportunities to think about fractional relationships. For example, they will be faced with measuring problems such as: what is half of 3 inches? what is one fourth of six inches? what is half of 1 and 1/2 inches? (Keep in mind that the squares will not be exactly 6" on a side when they are photocopied. Students will need to tolerate a bit of error in their measurements.)

Encourage students to make their final drafts as precise and clear as they can by using rulers to make their lines and by labeling the parts of their design with the appropriate fractions. Many students have invented ways of including sixteenths and even thirty-seconds and sixty-fourths (see figures 1.20 and 1.21).

If these problems are really too difficult for some students at this point in the unit, you may want to return to this activity later, after students have some experience with Modules 2, 3, and 4.

A final problem: Fraction relationships

Once students' squares are completed, write on the chalkboard:

$$1/4 = 2/8$$

Can any of you prove this using your squares?

Students volunteer to show how their squares can prove this equivalence. Can this be proven with all the squares, or are some more suited to this particular equation than others?

What are some other equations you can demonstrate with your square? What are some ways of making a whole that you can show with your square?

Ask students for examples like the one given above as well as examples of ways of making 1 which their squares illustrate, such as:

$$1 = 2/8 + 1/2 + 1/4$$

After some discussion, ask students to write facts about fractions which they can demonstrate on their own square. These may range from single equivalents:

$$1/4 = 2/8$$

to strings of equivalents:

$$1/2 = 2/4 = 4/8$$

to equations that include addition:

$$1/4 + 1/4 + 1/4 = 3/4$$
$$1/4 + 2/8 = 1/2$$
$$1/2 + 1/2 = 2/4 + 4/8$$

to equations showing different ways of making a whole:

$$1/2 + 1/2 = 1$$
$$1/4 + 2/8 + 4/8 = 1$$
$$1 = 1/4 + 1/4 + 1/4 + 1/4$$

As you circulate among the students, challenge them to include equations of all the types shown above. Ask students how they can prove that their equations work by using their square to demonstrate the relationships. Students' pages of equations should be included in their folder.

Examples of some student work are shown on the following pages (figures 1.20 and 1.21), after the two sample divisions of the large square.

Extension

In one class where students worked on the large 6" x 6" squares, each student chose her or his favorite square, made a good copy of it, and colored it. Then all the squares were put together into a large "quilt."

One way to divide the large square into halves, fourths, and eighths

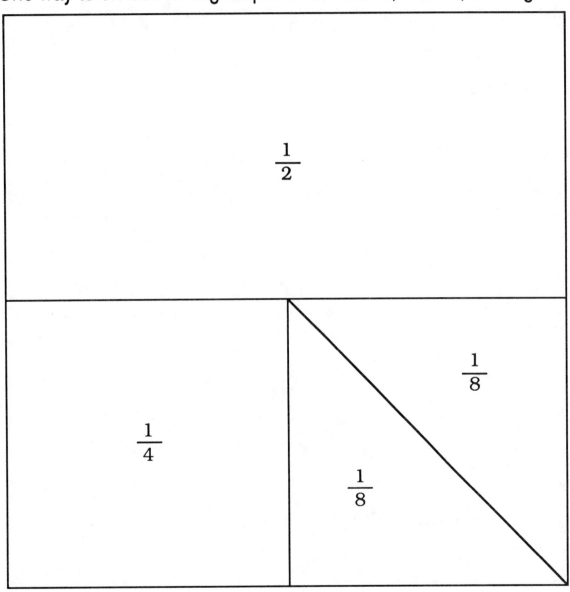

Figure 1.18

A division of the large square which includes sixteenths

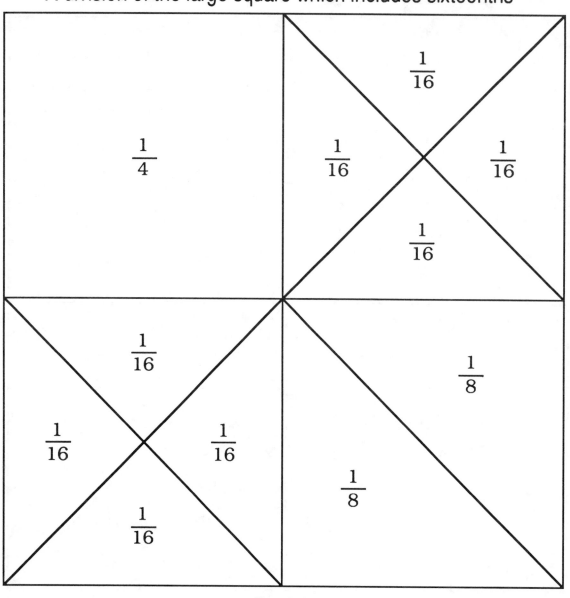

Figure 1.19

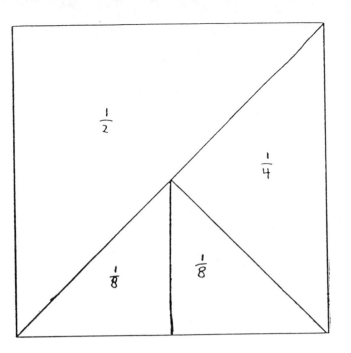

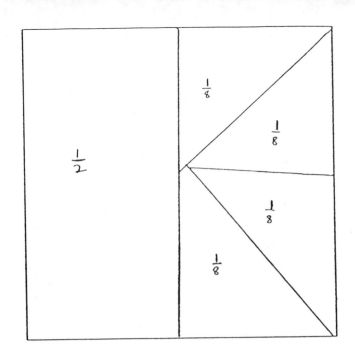

$$\frac{1}{2} = \frac{1}{4} + \frac{2}{8} \qquad \frac{1}{2} = \frac{1}{4} + \frac{1}{4} \qquad \frac{1}{2} = \frac{4}{16} + \frac{4}{16}$$

$$\frac{1}{2} = \frac{2}{8} + \frac{2}{8} \qquad \frac{1}{2} = \frac{2}{8} + \frac{2}{8} \qquad \frac{1}{2} = \frac{1}{2}$$

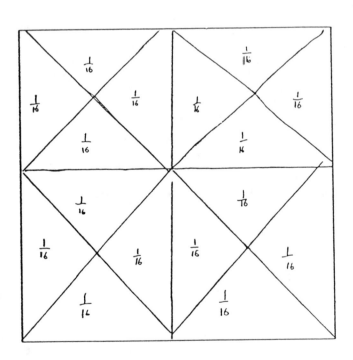

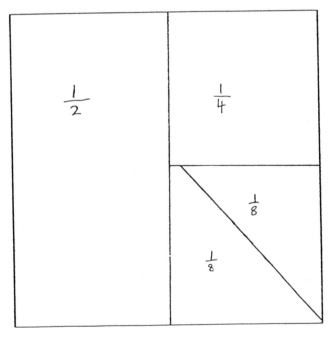

$$1 = \frac{1}{2} + \frac{1}{2} \qquad 1 = \frac{4}{8} + \frac{4}{8} \qquad 1 = \frac{2}{4} + \frac{2}{4}$$

$$1 = \frac{1}{2} + \frac{2}{4} \qquad 1 = \frac{8}{16} + \frac{8}{16}$$

$$1 = \frac{1}{2} + \frac{4}{8} \qquad 1 = \frac{1}{2} + \frac{1}{4} + \frac{2}{8}$$

Figure 1.20

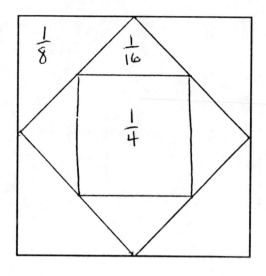

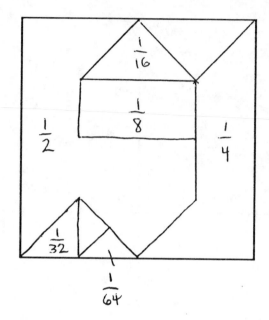

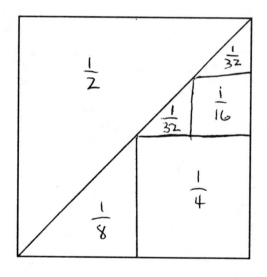

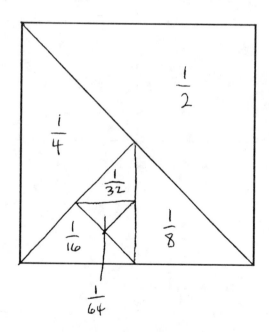

Figure 1.21

SESSIONS 5 AND 6 ACTIVITIES

In Sessions 5 and 6, students work on additions to their folders which demonstrate thirds, sixths, and twelfths:

First, using Worksheet 1.3 (6 x 4 squares), they show thirds in as many ways as they can. As before, small groups or pairs work together to generate many possibilities; then each child makes a page of thirds for his or her folder.

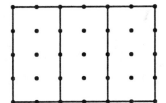 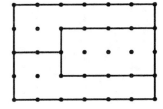

Figure 1.22

Then students make a page for sixths and one for twelfths, following the same procedures.

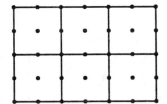 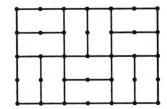

Figure 1.23

Using the 6" x 6" large squares or the 6 x 4 dot squares, each student makes a design which includes thirds, sixths, and twelfths, labels the parts (and colors the design, if desired), and writes a page showing equations demonstrated by this square.

These sessions proceed in the same way as the sessions on halves, fourths, and eighths. However, constructing thirds and sixths will be much more difficult for many students at this level. It is critical that students talk with each other and that, as you circulate among groups, you ask students to explain their approaches (see the TEACHER NOTE: "There's no other way to make sixths.").

Extensions

Select a couple of completed sixths and thirds made by students and challenge other students to prove that they are, in fact, sixths or thirds: "Can you prove that Alice's square is divided into sixths?" Students can write and illustrate their explanations.

Ask students to find halves, fourths, and eighths, using Worksheet 1.3. This activity can help them see that the size of a fraction changes when the size of the whole changes: while a fourth was four squares on Worksheet 1.1, it will be six squares on Worksheet 1.3.

A final challenge for some students is to combine halves, thirds, fourths, sixths, and eighths in one design on a 4" by 6" rectangle. This activity can also be saved for later in the unit.

TEACHER NOTE: "THERE'S NO OTHER WAY TO MAKE SIXTHS"

In one group of fifth grade students, most small groups quickly found these two ways to divide the rectangle into thirds and sixths:

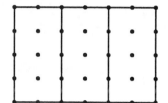 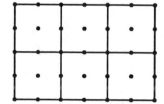

Figure 1.24

However, some groups were stuck and could go no further, even though they had successfully made irregular fourths and eighths in the previous sessions. As one student said, looking at his drawing, "There's no other possible way to make sixths." They seemed to have forgotten what their teacher thought they had already learned!

Students are so used to seeing illustrations of fractions in which squares or circles are divided up in regular ways that they have strong visual images about fractional pieces looking like small rectangles or slices of a pie. Even though they may be able to say that thirds do not have to look the same, it can still be difficult for them to visualize alternatives.

In attempting to find other ways to make thirds, students may appear to lose some of the important ideas about fractions which you thought they had internalized during the previous sessions. For example, even though they seemed to know that halves, fourths, and eighths were equal parts of a whole, some students may come up with designs like these for thirds:

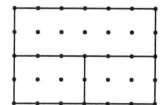 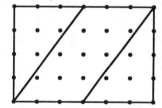

Figure 1.25

Don't despair! Students will need to meet these ideas over and over again in different contexts. Do you notice how, when you are trying to learn something new which is difficult, you seem to lose hold of some of the easy things you thought you already knew? This also happens to students as they encounter a familiar idea in a new context. This unit is designed for students to view the same ideas from different angles and to build a more thorough knowledge about the ideas by constantly using different models for different problems.

Simply support students in doing the same kind of thinking they did during the sessions on halves, fourths, and eighths. How do they know their design shows thirds? How can they prove it? When they were stuck and could not find any more halves, what were some of the strategies that worked? Can those strategies help them find sixths?

Sometimes students will work their way out of their dilemma by collaborating and helping each other with ideas. Working together, Cally and Alice were initially frustrated. They had come up with two ways of making thirds but could not think of any other ways:

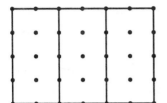 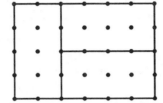

Figure 1.26

Cally remarks, "There's nothing else you can do with it. Just change it around a little bit." Alice replies, "I don't like odd numbers. They're dumb. Odd numbers are too hard."

They persevere, and finally Cally remembers about counting the squares for her irregular fourths: "It's eight squares; we can do it any way as long as there's eight squares." Once they have remembered that the pieces must have an equal area, they quickly come up with several more solutions:

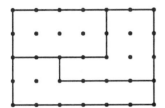 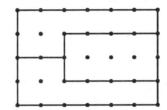

Figure 1.27

Alice becomes excited too. When they go on to sixths, Alice remarks, "I know! You count the squares." And Cally says, "It has to be one half of the thirds." Alice: "I still don't like odd numbers." Cally: "But with sixths, you'll be back to even numbers." Soon Alice is concentrating on dividing her thirds in half to make sixths.

It is often worthwhile to allow students to handle their own frustrations for a time so that they have a chance to find their own solutions. However, some students will be genuinely stuck and need your support. Some students became confused about *counting dots* as opposed to *counting squares*. In one group, the students had made the following thirds:

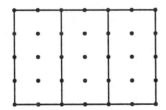 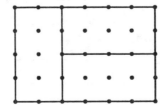

Figure 1.28

How do you know those are thirds?

Maria: We counted the dots.

After Maria demonstrated that she was counting the inside and perimeter dots for each part, the teacher remarked:

But some of the dots are part of two different rectangles.

Maria: That doesn't matter. It's still the same number of dots.

OK. Now what about Alice's and Cally's strategy, counting the squares? Does that work for yours?

Maria: Yeah, that works, too [Maria demonstrates].

I don't know if they're always the same. Could you try your method with a couple of Alice's thirds and see if it works?

After Maria and Alice compared strategies, they found that thirds with the same number of squares did not always have the same number of dots. Maria decided that she could trust squares, but not dots, because "squares always makes it fair, like if it was a candy bar." (However, she also continued trying to figure out how the dots could be related to the pieces. This is a difficult and intriguing problem which a few students may want to pursue.) Like Cally, Maria had noticed that the areas of the pieces have to be equivalent.

While making thirds and sixths may be a difficult task, it leads students to construct firmer ideas about the relationships among sixths and thirds and about the nature of fractional parts. During this work, listen for interesting discoveries or strategies which students invent. You may want to share these with the whole class. For example, one student who was working on thirds started with this pattern:

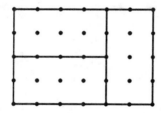

Figure 1.29

He then invented the following strategy: "If you cover up the rectangle on the side, then you have the squares, like we used before, so just do halves. You can use all your old halves ways, then uncover the other rectangle and you have thirds!":

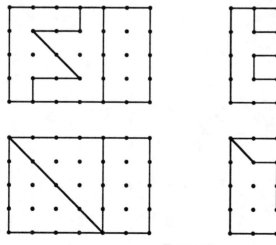

Figure 1.30

Module 1: Geometry with fractions

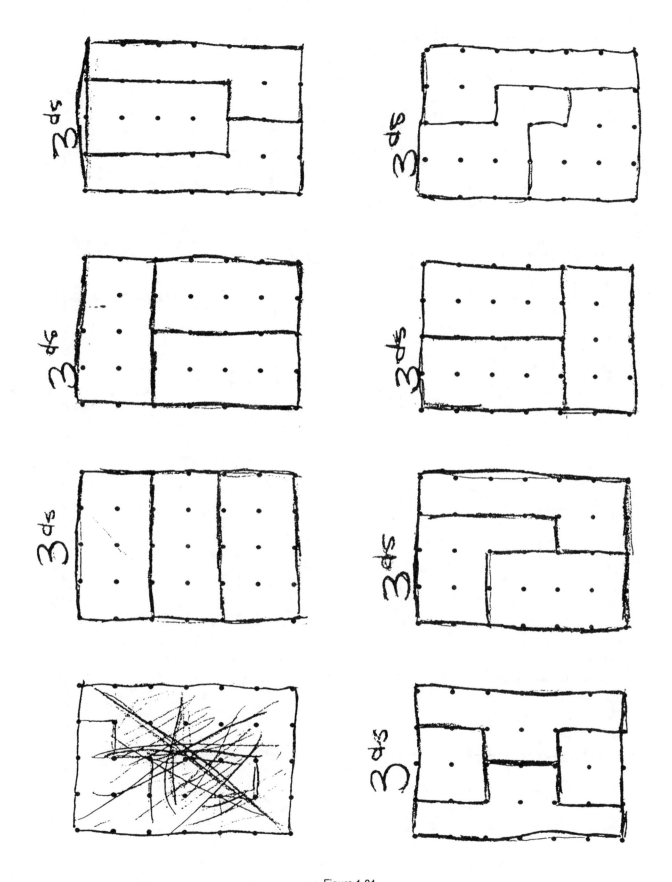

Figure 1.31

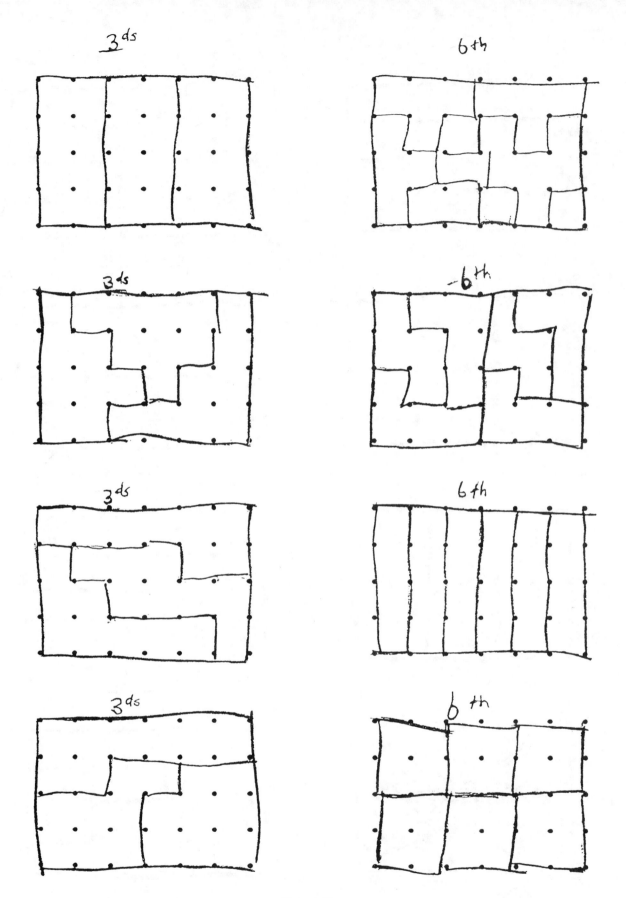

Figure 1.32

Module 1: Geometry with fractions

Figure 1.33

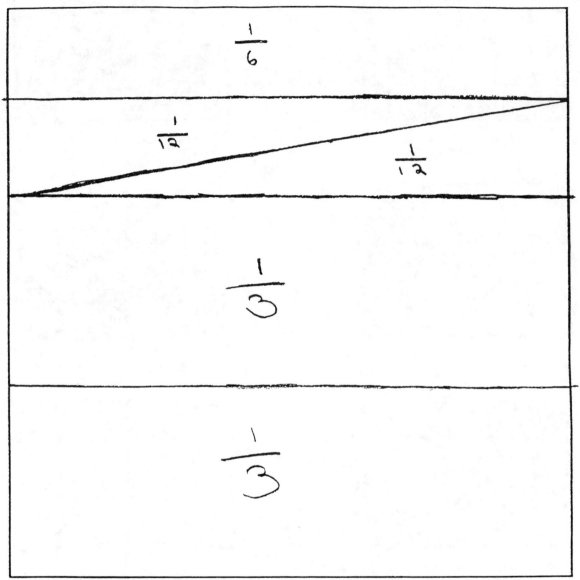

$$\frac{1}{3} + \frac{2}{6} = \frac{2}{3} \qquad \frac{1}{6} + \frac{1}{6} + \frac{1}{3} + \frac{1}{3} = 1 \qquad \frac{2}{12} + \frac{2}{6} = \frac{3}{6}$$

$$\frac{1}{3} + \frac{2}{12} + \frac{1}{6} = \frac{4}{6} \qquad \frac{1}{12} + \frac{1}{12} + \frac{1}{3} + \frac{1}{3} = \frac{5}{6} \qquad \frac{1}{6} + \frac{1}{6} = \frac{1}{3}$$

$$\frac{1}{3} + \frac{1}{3} + \frac{1}{3} = 1 \qquad \frac{1}{6} + \frac{1}{6} + \frac{1}{6} + \frac{1}{6} = \frac{2}{3} \qquad \frac{1}{3} + \frac{1}{3} = \frac{2}{3}$$

Figure 1.34

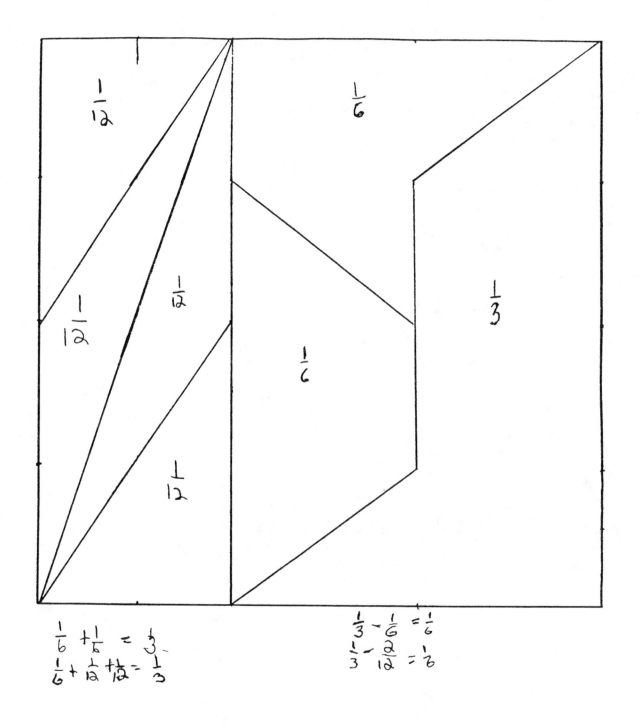

Figure 1.35

ANOTHER OPTION:
A TRIANGLE DESIGN

Some students may enjoy experimenting with a large equilateral triangle
(Worksheet 1.4) to make a design showing fractional parts. One example of
a completed design is provided (Figure 1.36). There are many other
possibilities. To get started, students should divide each side of the triangle
into halves or thirds, then connect these points. Some students used paper
folding to solve this problem. By folding the tip of the triangle down to its
base, then folding the left and right vertices into the middle of the base, the
triangle can be divided into fourths.

One way to divide the triangle into fourths, eighths, and sixteenths.

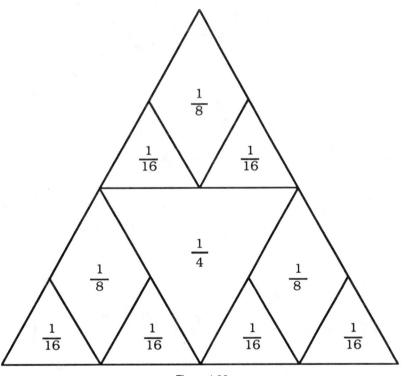

Figure 1.36

Module 1: Geometry with fractions

SOME POSSIBILITIES
FOR ASSESSMENT

This module focuses on using an area model of part-whole relationships to develop two key ideas—that equal fractions represent equal parts of a whole but that these same-sized parts may not look the same—and to familiarize students with basic relationships among common fractions—for example, that a fourth is half of a half. You have been engaged in assessing student understanding throughout these activities by observing them work, talking with them about their strategies, and looking at their finished products. Take some time before you start the next module to write a few comments about what you have learned about each student in your class. This record will serve to help you focus in different ways on what different students need during the next modules and, once they have completed the entire unit, your notes will help you document the changes you observed in their understanding.

Two additional types of problems you can use to assess how comfortable students are becoming with these ideas are the following:

❑ Draw several copies of an irregular dot shape, such as one of those shown below, and ask students to divide each copy into different fractions (one into halves, one into thirds, one into fourths, and so forth). Let them choose which fractions to use and challenge them to do as many of the different fractions they encountered in this module as they can. Shapes with 12 or 24 squares allow students to divide them evenly into halves, thirds, fourths, and sixths.

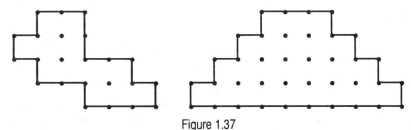

Figure 1.37

❑ Ask students to create an irregular dot shape of their own which can be divided into both halves and thirds (or both fourths and sixths) by connecting dots. Encourage students to experiment in order to decide for themselves what the areas of their shapes should be.

WORKSHEET 1.1

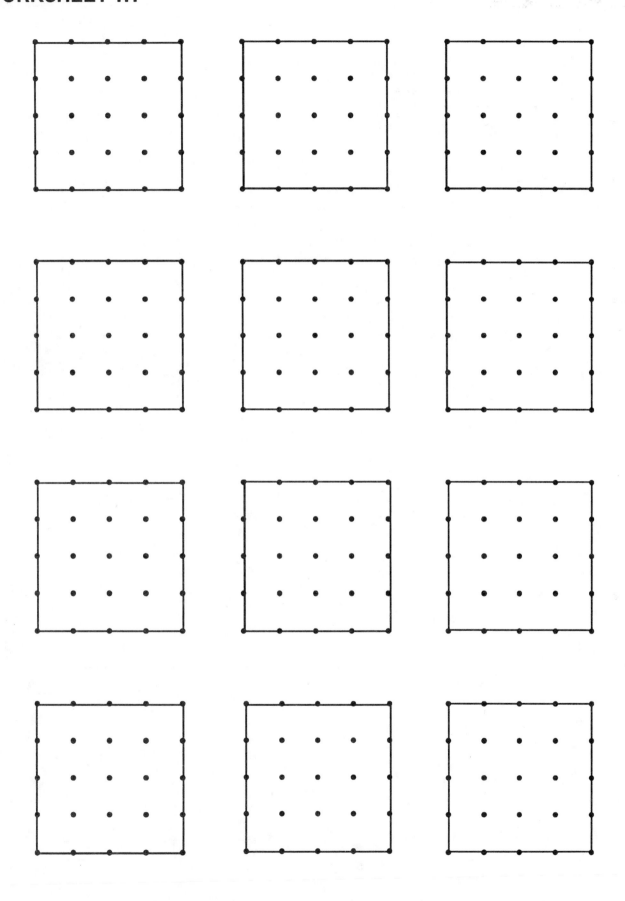

WORKSHEET 1.2

WORKSHEET 1.3

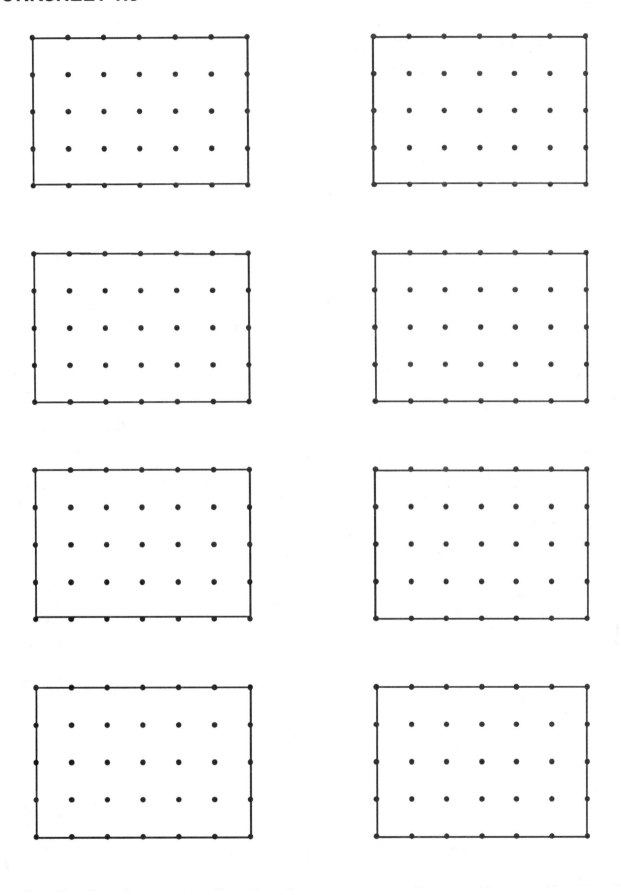

WORKSHEET 1.4

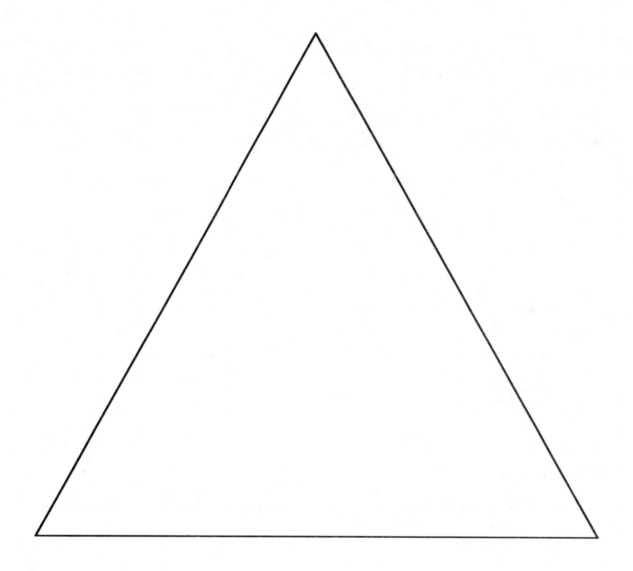

Module 2: Rates— a different model

MODULE OVERVIEW

WHAT HAPPENS

Rates are a common way of stating a relationship between two quantities. Fractional parts of a whole are one kind of relationship; the rate at which some quantity is repeated or generated or used is another. A rate is a fraction because it also expresses a relationship between two numbers. The manipulation and interpretation of rates provides a context that helps some students to understand the numerical relationships better than traditional part-whole models.

In this module, students use rates as a context for exploring fraction equivalents. After the teacher introduces a representation of a rate (4 peaches for 79¢ becomes 4/79), students search for examples of rates in the newspaper and work in small groups, building models of rates and solving some introductory rate problems.

Comparison problems are a common application of rates (for instance, knowing which is a better buy, 3 candies for 4¢ or 5 candies for 7¢). Students compare rates by generating series of equivalent rates, looking for an element common to them (in the case above, comparing 21 candies for 28¢ with 20 candies for 28¢), deciding which is the better buy. Students research local rates by collecting data on a selected topic, studying those data, and analyzing their real life "best buys."

After exploring number patterns and testing them for generalizability, students predict to find terms in a series of rates: If I know that 3 pens cost $5, how much will 12 cost? Finally, students search for a simpler rate, or base rate, in a rate that is not simplified.

This module is planned to take seven sessions of about 45 minutes each.

WHAT TO PLAN AHEAD OF TIME

❑ Decide how best to demonstrate materials to the class. You might use the overhead projector, or the chalkboard, or put materials on a table if everyone can see (Sessions 1 and 2).

❑ For Session 1, read the TEACHER NOTE: About rates and fractions and the TEACHER NOTE: What are rates? For Session 2, read the TEACHER NOTE: Comparing rates: Which is better? And for Session 5, read the TEACHER NOTE: Finding patterns in number series.

❑ Bring in newspapers so your students can search for examples of familiar rates. Think of some rates that involve your class directly, such

---

as sneakers per class or earrings per ear (for one student's ear). You
may also get some local statistics, such as the rate of tomato sauce
used in the cafeteria per week. Collect newspapers for a week or so for
your students to look through to find rates. Rates pop up in many
contexts— as crime rates, insurance rates, birth rates, illness rates
(Session 1).

❑ Provide macaroni, fake coins, and dice for each group of students. You
may want to use other materials as long as they are rather small. One
should be round to represent coins; the other should be nonrolling
(Sessions 1–7).

❑ Have calculators routinely available to students to solve problems
(Sessions 2–7).

❑ Provide copies of Worksheet 2.1 (Session 1), Worksheet 2.2 (Session 2),
and Worksheet 2.3 (Session 7).

❑ Allow time between Sessions 3 and 4 to collect data.

IMPORTANT MATHEMATICAL IDEAS

**Understanding the notion of a rate as a relationship between two
quantities.** Once a relationship between two quantities is established, all
different representations of this relationship are equivalent.

Generating the members of a series related to a particular base rate. If
candies are selling at 3 for 5¢, you can buy 6 for 10¢ and 30 for how
much? Three for 5¢ and 6 for 10¢ are members of the same series of rates.
The notion of building and recording a series is basic to students' later
comparison of rates to find "best buys."

Predicting a particular term in a series. Number patterns embedded in a
series of equivalent rates allow us to predict a particular term in that
series. That allows students an alternative way of thinking about
equivalents by analyzing and applying number pattern rules.

Making, explaining, and defending a mathematical prediction.
Predicting outcomes according to a number pattern is an important part of
mathematical work. These activities provide students the chance to make a
prediction and articulate their reasons for their conjecture.

Using materials and concrete models to show and defend a theory.
Materials are used to build models of rates and to generate representations
of series. Students use these materials to increase their understanding and
to explain and illustrate their thinking about their work.

Comparing two rates to find out which is more "expensive." The
process of rate comparison involves finding a common element and
comparing the other elements to determine which is the better value. For
instance, if you have one lollipop for three cents and four for nine cents,
which costs more? If you generate equivalents (1/3, 2/6, 3/9, 4/12, ...)
(4/9, 8/18, ...), you can find a point at which there is a common element
for each rate (in this example, you could use 3/9 vs. 4/9 to compare the
amount received for a given cost, or 4/12 vs. 4/9 to compare the cost of a
given amount).

SESSION 1 ACTIVITIES

Introduction: What are rates?

Bring in some newspaper examples of rates—rates in stores, rents, car payments, and any other rates you find as examples. You may want to make an overhead projector transparency for some of these.

During the introduction to rates, write them on the overhead or chalkboard as they are mentioned. For some ideas, see the TEACHER NOTE: About rates and fractions.

We talk about rates often. A babysitter sets his or her rates at so much an hour. We talk about miles per hour, cans of cat food for a dollar, dollars for a pound. A babysitter might charge $4.50 *per* hour and write it as *$4.50 / hour*. When we say 50 miles *per* hour, we could write *50 miles / hour*. Three cans for a dollar can be represented as *3 cans / dollar*. Fruit that's selling for 79¢ for 2 pounds can be written as *79¢ / 2 pounds* or *2 pounds / 79¢*. What are some examples of rates you can think of?

Ask students for their ideas of rates. In some classes, students mentioned car payments ($125 per month) and rent ($600 per month) as examples. Your students' knowledge may surprise you.

After your students have come up with some ideas of their own, pass out newspapers and ask each small group to find as many rates as they can.

Let's look through these newspapers and find some examples of rates we can put on the board for everyone.

Students write down examples of rates so that they can report to the large group. Spend about ten minutes combing the newspapers. The timing may vary, though. In some classes students have become deeply involved in this activity and have spent a whole session discussing and comparing the rates they found.

When you feel that this discussion has produced enough examples and when your students seem ready, turn to the materials and use them to introduce the concept of a base rate and a rate series. Make sure that each group has a container of the "coins" and other markers you will be using during this session.

Orientation to the model: Setting a base rate and generating a series

I found a real bargain at a flea market. I bought a tremendous box of individually wrapped hard candies—lots of different flavors. My idea is to sell them in packages of 5 candies for 2¢. [Write the rate 5/2 on the board.] If you want to buy ten, how much money do you have to give me? If you want to buy fifteen?

Leave time for your students to think about this problem and to show ways of solving it. Talk with them about their methods, making sure that they clarify the thinking behind each method.

I want to show you one way to think about this—a way of generating a series
of rates to represent this kind of problem.

Figure 2.1

Ask students to build a concrete model of this rate, working with the
person next to them— five macaronis to stand for the candies, two coins for
the 2¢. Ask them to build another rate packet of 5 candies for 2¢— and
another— and another— and another.

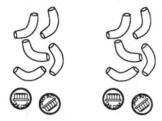

Figure 2.2

As we build these packets, think about what they mean. The first one I will
sell at a rate of five for 2¢. After I sell the second one, what will be the total
I've sold? And after the third packet? And after the fourth? And after the
fifth? How many candies will I have sold in all after I've sold five packets?
How much money will I have gotten from selling five packets?

Record it as a number series:

$$\left\{ \frac{5}{2}, \frac{10}{4}, \frac{15}{6}, \frac{20}{8}, \frac{25}{10}, \ldots \right\}$$

Let's see what you think would happen if we sold *another* packet. That's a
total of 6 packets all together. How many candies would I have sold if I sold
six packets of candies? How much money in all would I have taken in?

Ask students to share the reasoning behind their predictions. There may
be different ways of thinking of this problem. Try another problem to make
sure that this model is solid for your students:

I found a vending machine that dispenses peanuts for 4 pennies. I got seven
peanuts each time. After I used the machine six times, let's look at how many
peanuts I've gotten and how much money it cost me to get them.

The *base rate* is 7 peanuts/4¢. Work in your groups. Build a model and record
the rate series on this paper. We'll compare notes when you've finished.

Ask students to use Worksheet 2.1 to build and record their models. When
students are done, have them tell you what the base rate is and what the
first five (or six or seven) terms in the series are. Ask for frequent
explanations and take this slowly. What is the sixth term? How much
money do these six transactions cost? How many peanuts do you get for
that money?

You may want to have students continue working with rate problems that are provided to them; you may prefer to have them generate some of their own problems. The next two sections present options for you.

Solving some rate problems: Using materials (Option one)

If you choose to have your students continue working with rate problems, building models of the base rate and then subsequent packets of materials based on that rate, here are four more problems for them to work with:

❏ I had such success selling candies at 5 for 2¢ that I decided to raise my prices. Now I'm going to sell 5 candies for 4¢. How much did I get at the first rate for 40 candies? How much do I get now for 40 candies?

❏ Sandy runs seven miles a day in the morning. How far does he run in six days? Show this and solve it as a rate and in other ways.

❏ Jesse bought some new sneakers. He had to borrow money from his big sister. She wants him to pay her back $15 every two weeks. He borrowed $90. How long will he have to pay her back?

❏ Suellen wanted to collect a lot of pennies, so she planned to sell her two lunch cookies for 12¢ each day to a sixth grader who promised to pay in pennies. How many pennies will she have after he buys 30 cookies?

Writing rate problems: Making sense of the model (Option two)

You may prefer to have your students collectively write some rate problems. Take a rate as an example and ask the class to make up some problems, using that rate. Record the problems on the overhead or the chalkboard under that rate. Wait until you have two or three problems recorded before you go on to the small-group work.

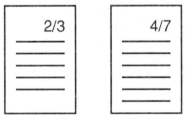

Ask students to suggest two or three base rates (such as 4 for 7) and record each one on the top of a big piece of newsprint paper, on the top of an overhead projector transparency, or in a space of its own on the chalkboard. These spaces will be used to record the problems the students generate. In small groups, have students make up problems that are based on the rates they selected. When the small groups have finished, ask them to share their problems with the group. Record the problems under the base rates they illustrate. Solve one or two with the class and compare possible solution strategies.

TEACHER NOTE: WHAT ARE RATES?

We do not always think of rates as part of the study of fractions. The models used in school typically show how fractions describe parts of objects (3/4 of a pizza) or groups (3/4 of the class of 24 students). These are specific instances of fractions, but there are other situations in which fractional notation is used to indicate a different kind of relationship between two numbers.

A rate describes a series of ratios in which a number of one kind of thing has a constant relationship to another kind of thing. If 3 tomatoes are sold for 80¢, then the rate expressing this relationship between tomatoes and money is 3 tomatoes for 80¢ and can be written as 3/80. For a larger number of tomatoes, say 6, the cost goes up according to this established rate. Six tomatoes cost $1.60, and 6/1.60 is an expression of the same rate. Rates need not be about price. A walker who burns 80 calories per quarter hour knows that he or she will continue to burn calories at the same rate. In half an hour, he or she will have burned 160 calories, or 160 calories/2 quarter hours.

Many everyday ratios are rates. Rates of speed (55 miles per hour), costs (24 baseball cards for $2.49), and production rates (4 light bulbs per minute) are all ways of demonstrating those relationships. They are used to help us predict totals and to look beyond the current situation and figure an amount that is not given. If a light bulb manufacturer makes 4 light bulbs per minute, that company can figure how many bulbs to expect to make in one day. Four per minute is the same rate as 240 in an hour and so on.

The advantage of rates is that one pair of numbers can tell us about an infinite number of situations. We compute to find the particular situation we are interested in. If you know that you get 9 M&Ms from a vending machine for a quarter, you may want to compare that with the cost of a small pack of M&Ms. In that case, the rate of 9 for 25¢ is a base rate that establishes the relationship between M&Ms and their cost. You can use that information to find more information about equivalents to that base rate.

$$\frac{9}{25} = \frac{18}{50} = \frac{27}{75} = \frac{36}{100}$$

Finding those equivalents helps you compare. Determining that you get 36 M&Ms from the machine for $1.00 helps you make decisions about whether to buy a bag of 40 candies at 79¢ instead of using the machine.

Using fractions to model rates allows students to work with equivalence in ways they may not have envisioned before. Number patterns generated from this model help in future problems, and finding numerical patterns can be exciting, creative, and generative for students who like to find and predict outcomes of number work.

For some students, using a rate model is freeing. They can find equivalents using many strategies that may not seem evident to them when working only with part-whole fraction models.

TEACHER NOTE: ABOUT RATES AND FRACTIONS

One of the confusing aspects of fractional notation is that the symbols themselves can stand for different real-life situations. When we see 3/5, it may be a part/whole model of a fraction:

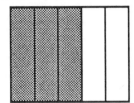 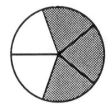

Figure 2.3

Or it may represent a rate:

$3.00 for 5 pens (or $3 / 5 pens)

Or the ratio of red socks to blue socks in my drawer:

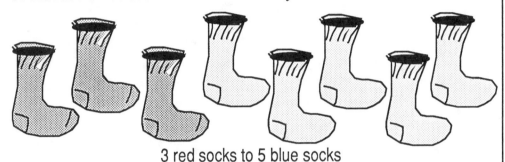

3 red socks to 5 blue socks

Figure 2.4

These examples are all described by the same symbol (3/5), even though the situations they represent look quite different. We have a fraction of three pieces out of five pieces, that is, 3 pieces of the 5 equal pieces that make the whole. We have a rate of $3 for every five pens, that is, a constant relationship of $3 for every 5 pens. We have the ratio of three red socks to five blue socks, that is, a particular relationship comparing the colors of socks in my drawer. Each of these is a relationship of 3 things to or out of 5 things. Each of these is represented as 3/5.

The fractions describing these situations are not read in the same way. The line that separates the upper and lower terms is read differently. In a rate, it's "three for every five" or "three per five." In a part-whole model, it's "three-fifths" or 3 out of 5 pieces.

When working with the part-whole representation of fractions to find equivalents and compare fractions, students must keep in mind the complex relationship of parts and wholes while remembering that having more pieces means having smaller pieces.

Working with rates as a model involves generating repeated examples of a rate. Rather than cutting something into ever smaller pieces, students work with materials to generate more and more "packets" of the base rate. This alternative model is one that some students find easier to use to generate equivalent fractions and to compare unequal fractions.

SESSION 2 ACTIVITIES

Comparisons and equivalents

This session focuses on finding patterns that allow students to generate series and to find equivalent rates. Again, the concrete model will be used as the basis of the work. Hand out the materials to students as they are seated in the whole group and ask them to work the problem with the materials.

I was at the amusement park last Saturday. I bought gumballs from one machine—I got 3 gumballs for eight pennies. My friend JoAnne told me that she'd found a different machine where gumballs were 12 for twenty cents. How could we compare them to find out which was the better buy?

Support your students as they try to find ways of solving that problem. Some will instinctively build concrete models; others will want to work with the numbers. Ask them to share their solution strategies with the whole class. Make sure that students can talk through their strategies with reference to the physical model, although there are other strategies that work well (see the TEACHER NOTE: Comparing rates: Which is better?).

After your students have demonstrated and defended their methods, show them that you can compare rates by looking for equivalents in the rate series and finding terms you can compare. Record the relevant series on the chalkboard:

$$\left\{ \frac{3}{8}, \frac{6}{16}, \frac{9}{24}, \frac{12}{32}, \frac{15}{40}, ... \right\}$$

and

$$\left\{ \frac{12}{20}, \frac{24}{40}, ... \right\}$$

When you have fractions with a common element (for example, 15 for 40 and 24 for 40), you can compare them to see which is a better deal.

Students enjoy comparison problems a great deal, although some are confused momentarily by the fact that equivalence can arise in different terms in each rate series. In this gumball problem, the equivalents come in the fifth term of one series and the second of another. But which machine would you rather put your money in? As one student observed, "The term only tells you how often you have to put money into the machine. It doesn't matter how often you do and how much time it takes. You want to find the one where you get the most for the money, no matter if it takes a short or a long time at each machine."

Doing comparison problems in small groups

Ask students to try some other comparison problems. We have included four on Worksheet 2.2. You might decide to focus on only one or two of the problems. As students work in their small groups, circulate and ask them about their methods and their models. Most students should still be using materials to generate rate packets for comparison.

Playing with rates: Finding the better buy

If your students have time, they can play a simple game to compare two rates. They need two dice (one each of two colors) and their rate-building materials.

Each student rolls the dice to get a rate. So, for example, one student might roll a 2 and a 3 and can establish her rate as 2 for 3 (or 3 for 2). Another student might roll a 1 and a 5 and so can choose 1 for 5 (or 5 for 1) as her rate. If students roll 1/1 or another fraction equivalent to one, they roll again. Otherwise, they compare those two rates to find which is the better buy.

TEACHER NOTE: COMPARING RATES: WHICH IS BETTER?

If the Flavorite Candy Company has six red candies in every packet of thirty candies and the Licksalot Company has packets of forty candies with nine reds in them, which is better *if I like red candies?* Which is better if I prefer other flavors?

In order to compare two rates, students will invent a variety of methods. Generating sets of equivalents in similar problems helps students to find terms so that they can compare rates directly.

For instance, in the example above, these are the sets of equivalents:

$$\left\{ \frac{6}{30}, \frac{12}{60}, \frac{18}{90}, \frac{24}{120}, \frac{30}{150}, ... \right\} \text{ FLAVORITE}$$

and

$$\left\{ \frac{9}{40}, \frac{18}{80}, \frac{27}{120}, \frac{36}{160}, ... \right\} \text{ LICKSALOT}$$

When the two denominators are the same (at 24/120 and 27/120), comparison is possible. You get 24 reds for every 120 Flavorite candies but 27 reds for the same number of Licksalot candies. When the two numerators are the same (at 18/90 and 18/80), comparison is also possible. You have to buy fewer Licksalot candies than Flavorite candies in order to get 18 reds. When there's a clear reference point, comparison is easy.

Other methods work, too. Some students like to find the "cost" of one candy or one Ninja Turtle card and compare the two rates by using the cost per unit. If candies cost 5¢ for 4 candies in one store and 25¢ for 24 candies in another, some students want to find the cost per candy. In the first store, the cost is 1 1/4 cents per candy; in the second, it's 1.04¢ or 1 1/24 cents each. This makes a cost comparison very clear.

A few students have invented methods of finding common numerators in order to compare. In the example above, the 5/4 rate can also be expressed as 10/8, 15/12, 20/16, 25/20. Because we can tell now that those candies cost 25¢ for 20, we know that the other price, 25¢ for 24, is a better deal for us.

The method that's used is not crucial. The important thing is for your students to find some way of making the comparison concrete and comprehensible.

SESSION 3 ACTIVITIES

In our experiences: Rates in reality

Initiate a discussion with the whole class, eliciting their ideas about rates in their own lives.

Have you thought about ways rates make a difference in your real life?

Keep a list on the board as students bring up examples of rates in their own lives. Try to make sure that they are able to talk about some examples that are not based only on money. If they don't, you might bring some in yourself.

Do you think you all pay the same prices for New Kids on the Block cards or Teenage Mutant Ninja Turtles cards? They may be sold at different rates.

Doing research on rates

We can collect data on these topics so that we can compare them in real life. How could we do that?

Pick some examples the students have mentioned during the discussion—they may involve one of the latest fads. When this module was written, the fad collector's items were baseball cards, Teenage Mutant Ninja Turtles cards, and New Kids on the Block cards. They were sold at many different rates. Baseball cards, particularly, varied in rate, making them a good candidate for a research project. Students paid very different amounts for different numbers of cards, depending on the source.

Another possibility is babysitting rates and rates students charge for other jobs. How do they figure their babysitting rates? Do they compare? Are they different when they take care of "frequent users" of their services? What are the rates they charge for other jobs? These may also vary a great deal. They may be very interested in thinking about comparisons here and what constitutes a "good deal" for them or for their customers.

How could we do some comparative research about these topics? What do we need in order to make some price comparisons?

Record students' ideas about collecting data in order to make some real life comparisons on topics they select. Be sure that they know exactly what information they need. They will be collecting data in between this session and the next one, so they need to be clear about what they need to get and do.

Now that you know what information to collect after school, let's decide how you'll get it and where.

Help students refine questions and decide how to collect data.

In order to be sure that the students will have enough data to make some comparisons, collect some information yourself, getting at least two pieces of data on each question the students selected.

SESSION 4 ACTIVITIES

Recording the research data

At the start of the class, ask students to record their data on the board. Under each of the topics being investigated, the students who found information write their data.

Divide the class into small groups to write, solve, and share their own problems using any or all of these data. Here are two examples written by fifth graders:

❑ One person in our class named Billy buys 5 baseball cards at the ice cream truck for 25¢, but here in the valley we can buy 16 baseball cards for 50¢. I said, Billy, you're getting 10 cards for 50¢. I said, Billy, you're getting cheated. You should find a cheaper card shop.

❑ You can buy juice packs at the supermarket in boxes of 12 for $1.70. At the convenience store on the corner near school, they sell the same brand for 65¢ for a three-pack. Which store offers you the better buy?

When the groups have finished writing their problems, ask the groups to illustrate the problems. The groups may want to read the problems aloud to share them with the rest of the class. You may want to bind the problems into a booklet to keep in the class library.

SESSION 5 ACTIVITIES

Looking for patterns: Brainstorming and pattern-finding

One of the exciting aspects of studying rates is the patterns equivalents make. Many students enjoy finding patterns in numbers and series. As they spot patterns in these series, make sure that they test them by predicting the next term in the series using their pattern and check it carefully to make sure that it works.

First, generate a series on the chalkboard.

Let's look at some of the patterns in a series of rates. They make it easy to predict terms and to work with series to solve problems. Someone suggest a base rate to explore.

Record the base rate and ask students to imagine the next term in the series. Generate five or six terms and ask students to think about them.

$$\left\{ \frac{4}{5}, \frac{8}{10}, \frac{12}{15}, \frac{16}{20}, \frac{20}{25}, \ldots \right\}$$

There are many, many patterns embedded in this series. For the next few minutes, describe the ones you can see. We'll list some of them and test one or two. Then you'll work in your small groups to find even more patterns.

Reflect on the series on the board. Wait for students to come up with patterns (for examples, see the TEACHER NOTE: Finding patterns in number series). As one or two patterns are suggested, test them on this series. See the DIALOGUE BOX: Does this pattern work?

Record students' patterns as they dictate them to you. Have the class check the patterns by using them to predict the next term and seeing whether the pattern "works" as a predictor. Some students may choose to use materials to illustrate or test their patterns, so they should be easily available. Make sure that you have students diagram or describe their patterns exactly. You may want to name the pattern for its discoverer—Alicia's Pattern, Ricardo's Pattern.

Testing patterns in rate series

Ask students to work in small groups. Each group explores a rate series they choose for themselves. They spend some time exploring their patterns, testing them, and recording them to share with the whole class.

Call students together to look at and share the results of their explorations. Make a master list of the patterns (in some cases a diagram works well) to keep for the next class, when you will test them for their general usefulness.

Some patterns are limited to one series. They work well for that one, but they don't help with others. In the next session we will look for patterns that work for many rates—maybe for all rate series.

TEACHER NOTE: FINDING PATTERNS IN NUMBER SERIES

Finding, testing, and formulating the patterns in number series is endlessly interesting for some students. Series of fractional equivalents can lead to some exciting discoveries.

When analyzing a series like

$$\left\{ \frac{2}{3}, \frac{4}{6}, \frac{6}{9}, \frac{8}{12}, \frac{10}{15}, \frac{12}{18}, ... \right\}$$

students begin to generate wonderful patterns:

❑ If you look at the fourth term, it's times four on the top and on the bottom and that's because it's fourth so it's four out from the base rate and that's what makes it times four because you take it four times.

❑ The fifth term is five out on the top, so you can count 2, 4, 6, 8, 10 up to five terms out and on the bottom 3, 6, 9, 12, 15 because that's five out too.

❑ It's because you're adding the base rate five times.

❑ The top number goes up slower than the bottom one, so the bottom one gets bigger faster.

❏ Every term is up by two on top and three on the bottom because it's one more of the base rate, and that's up by two coins and three macaronis.

❏ When you want to find the fourteenth term in the series, take the base rate fourteen times. So you take the top number times fourteen and the bottom number times fourteen because you are taking fourteen of them in the base rate.

If students don't work long enough with the materials, this kind of discovery can't take place.

When students make their own discoveries, the discoveries may look just like the conventional algorithm for finding equivalent fractions,

$$\frac{2 \times 5}{3 \times 5} = \frac{?}{15}$$

but students know what they are doing and why. They have discovered for themselves some reasons for the multiply-by-the-same-number-on-the-top-and-the-bottom rule. These patterns are much more likely to be discovered and understood when students have generated the series of equivalents from the materials.

If students have worked without reference to using the materials in previous sessions, they may skip terms because of taking mental shortcuts. One such speedy student generated the series,

$$\left\{ \frac{2}{5}, \frac{4}{10}, \frac{8}{20}, \frac{16}{40}, \dots \right\}$$

Then he said, "The only pattern I see is double it and double it. How come you get 6/15?" Leaving out the intermediate terms later compromised his ability to derive any interesting patterns for finding equivalent fractions. Instead of exploring the rich array of possibilities in the fully-expressed series,

$$\left\{ \frac{2}{5}, \frac{4}{10}, \frac{6}{15}, \frac{8}{20}, \frac{10}{25} \right\}$$

students who "skip terms" tend to find one and only one pattern in the series ("double the top number and double the bottom number too"). They easily fall victim to the magic of rote number-crunching.

In the words of one student: "At first I thought I knew how to do it. Um, for 10 you get 25. So maybe you divided it up into that and one of that is 2/5. What will go into 10 and 25? So you have to add...I can't do this. I don't know how to show it."

Contrast this with the words of another, who consistently used and referred to the materials: "Which is a better deal? Two cents for five macaronis or three cents for seven? Well, get it both to six cents and compare. That's easy to find. Just it looks better when you compare by finding the same amount of money because the amount of macaronis increases faster than the amount of cents. So the differences like show up better when you look at macaronis because they're more far apart from each other because the base rate has more."

DIALOGUE BOX: DOES THIS PATTERN WORK?

In this fifth grade classroom the students have been exploring patterns in the series {4/5, 8/10, 12/15, 16/20, 20/25...}. They have found many that appear to work. Jerry suggests his pattern:

Jerry: If you look at the 5 and then the eight, it's three apart. And then the ten is two apart from the eight. And then the twelve is another two. And then the twelve is three away from the fifteen. And it's one from the fifteen to the sixteen. So it goes three and then two and then two and then three and then one. And then...

And then the twenties...

Jerry: And then they are zero. Well...

Cindy: Well, I don't think it's a pattern, Jerry. It goes in jumps but they aren't in order and they don't repeat and all.

So, Cindy, are you saying that a pattern goes in order and something repeats?

Cindy: Something has to go over again or it's not a pattern. Like if it went 3, 2, 1 or something and then 3, 2, 1 again. Or something.

Let's go back to Jerry's pattern. Jerry, what do you think?

Jerry: It isn't a pattern. Because it goes by zero and then by five and then by one. It isn't. But I thought it was.

There are lots of times it looks like a pattern and then it isn't. There's nothing wrong with thinking one is—but it has to be tested.

This investigation led Jerry to decide he had been a bit premature in claiming he saw a pattern— and gave others the chance to test his pattern to see whether it held. Because his teacher did not insist on his being "correct"or "wrong," Jerry got the time to evaluate his "pattern" himself.

TEACHER NOTE: SOME STUDENT PATTERNS

This list of students' patterns is included to give you an idea of the variety of possible responses. Note that some of the patterns are generalizable, but some work only for one particular series. As you look through this list, you may want to think of ways of testing each pattern on another series.

❑ I noticed there was a pattern when trying to find the best deal in rates. Such as 4/5 = 8/10 = 12/15 = 16/20 = 20/25 and so on. Every time I add on more fractions, the denominator and numerator change forward or backwards by 1.

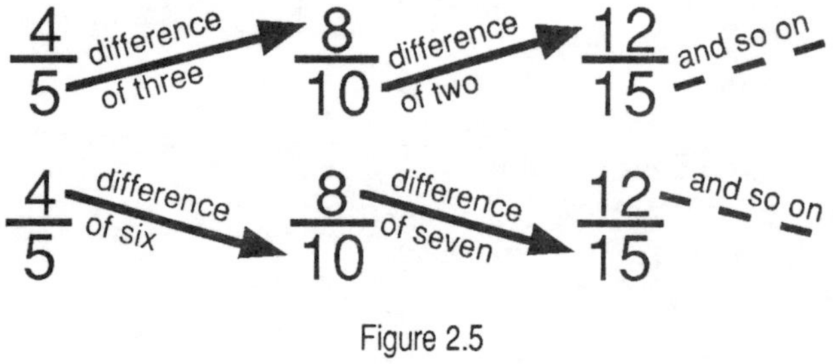

$$\frac{4}{5} \xrightarrow{\text{difference of three}} \frac{8}{10} \xrightarrow{\text{difference of two}} \frac{12}{15} \text{ and so on}$$

$$\frac{4}{5} \xrightarrow{\text{difference of six}} \frac{8}{10} \xrightarrow{\text{difference of seven}} \frac{12}{15} \text{ and so on}$$

Figure 2.5

❏ I looked at the rates, and I always see that the numerator goes up by the same amount as the base rate, and the denominator goes up by the same amount as the base rate. So when I have 2/3, I get 2/3; and then it's the base rate again, so it's 4/6; and then it's the base rate again, so it's 6/9.

❏ When we looked at the rates, we saw that the top number and the bottom number were only 3 apart at first in the base rate when we had 4/7. Then we got 8/14, and they were six apart. Then we got 12/21, and they were 9 apart. So every time it goes up by three. But it doesn't work on some other rates.

SESSION 6 ACTIVITIES

Testing patterns: Which work on more than one rate?

In the last session we found many patterns that work for these different rate series. But some patterns only work for one series. If we investigate these patterns, we can find some that work for many series. Those patterns allow you to predict terms for many series, not just one.

Let's try to test one of these patterns all together.

Choose one pattern that looks fairly straightforward. Ask students how to test its predictability with another series. Take their suggestions and try them with one or two other rate series. See whether they are generalizable for one or two series.

If you find one suggestion that looks broadly generalizable, try it on two or three other series. How well does it predict the patterns? Can it be used to find solutions to equivalence problems?

In your small groups, take this time to test the patterns and find some that look as though they work for more than one series.

Comparing notes: Which ones seem to generalize?

When students have found one or two patterns that are generalizable, ask the students to write about their findings.

Talk about your ideas with your group members and then write down what you found out. How did you test your ideas? How do you know they will generalize to more than one or two series?

Once students have written their rules, they may want to share them or talk about what they've found. Keep these papers as a piece of their mathematics portfolios if you are keeping such records of students' work.

TEACHER NOTE: GENERAL PATTERNS

Students will generate many, many patterns that show relationships between different parts of the rates. Many student patterns show relationships between numerators and denominators such as that below:

Figure 2.6

The differences between the numerators and denominators increase by three each time. However, this pattern does not work for other rate series (1/2, for instance, increases by one each time [1/2, 2/4, 3/6, 4/8]).

A more general pattern, on the other hand, relates the numerators and denominators of the terms to each other. In this case, the student noted that to get to the second term you "go up by two in the numerator and the denominator"; and to get to the third, you "go up by three times the base rate."

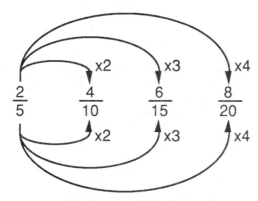

Figure 2.7

This pattern is generalizable. Although the outcomes are specific to this base rate, the pattern itself allows one to generate and predict any series.

In order to test a pattern for generalizability, suggest that students try it on different base rates, looking for confirming or denying evidence. Does it work for more than two rates? Does it hold in all cases?

The general patterns your students develop will allow them to predict and check rates as they look for equivalents. Having an underlying model will help many of your students find equivalents and simplify fractions.

SESSION 7 ACTIVITIES

Using patterns: Predicting and checking

Let's choose one base rate and predict the series, using the patterns you wrote about in the last session.

Generate a series from a base rate you roll with the dice. Have students predict the next term using a variety of the patterns they've identified.

Prediction strategies

I have a friend who earns two dollars for every three times she walks her parents' dog. She knows that this week she will walk the dog twelve times. How much will she earn?

$$\frac{2}{3} = \frac{?}{12}$$

Two per three is equivalent to how many *per* twelve?

Allow time for students to think about the problem and ask students to talk about their strategies. Expect responses like the following:

❑ Find how many out from the base rate it is. Like here it's the fourth one out. Then take the fourth one out on the top number because they're the same rate.

❑ Take the rate that's there and then keep making more of it until you get the number the same as you need it. Like 4/6, 6/9, 8/12, then twelve is the same between them, and so stay there.

Making and testing predictions

With the class, generate one series of equivalent rates on the board and use it to demonstrate a prediction/proof problem.

Sometimes it's much faster to know some definite ways of predicting to a particular place in a rate.

$$\left\{ \frac{3}{5}, \frac{6}{10}, \frac{9}{15}, \frac{12}{20}, \frac{15}{25}, \dots \right\}$$

We have generated these terms in the series. Can you find the sixth term? The tenth term? The hundredth term? You've talked about patterns for predicting. Let's try them out.

Ask your students to find these terms and to talk about methods. How do they do these problems? How could they prove they were right?

Can you find the seventh member of the rate family 3/4? Use your best method and let's see what you get. How did you think about it? How did you do it?

Ask another of the same type.

Can you find the fifth member of the series based on 1/7?

List students' methods on the board. There are many, many possibilities for problems: Set your class some problems to solve in their small groups. You may want to use Worksheet 2.3. As the groups work, make sure that materials are easily accessible to build rate models.

Predicting backwards to a base rate: Simplifying the numbers

Jorge bought 12 pieces of gum for 40¢. Sandra wants some, too, but doesn't have 40¢. What's the least money it would cost her to get some gum?

Ask students how to solve this problem. Record their strategies on the board so that they can be shared. Some students may use materials and others will not. Make sure that the materials are available for those who want to use them.

Set students a much harder problem, simplifying rates to find the base rate.

What if someone asked you to do a problem like this:

Sandra is interested in buying party favors for the friends she is inviting to her birthday party. The price of the fancy straws she wants is 12¢ for 20 straws. The storekeeper is willing to split a bundle of straws for her. She wants thirty-five straws. How much will they cost?

Build a concrete model of the rate 12/20. Ask each small group to build the model, too. Now, using the materials, ask them all to try to solve the problem.

You may want to write this on the board as:

$$\frac{12}{20} = \frac{?}{35}$$

Ask the groups to develop a strategy using the materials first and then the numbers. Ask students to share their methods with the whole class and see whether they are aware when they are finding the simplest form of the rate. Ask them to share patterns and to compare what they are doing here with what they did earlier.

One more similar problem will let students think again about solution strategies:

Ricardo bought baseball cards at Walworth's. He got 10 for $1.20. LeAnn bought some baseball cards, too, but she got 15 for $1.95. Who got the better deal? Find some ways of comparing these rates.

Writing about method

Writing about these methods in mathematics journals is a way students can consolidate their thinking and explore their ideas. Students find ways of drawing and writing about mathematics that help them to understand their own thoughts and help us gain some insight. Here are two examples from student journals:

❑ You know that 12¢ buys 20 straws. How many cents do you need for 35 straws? We think that 27 cents gets you 35 straws because if you take 12 cents and subtract it from 20 straws you get 8, and so we take 8 from 35 straws and got 27 cents.

❑ I think 3 cents for 5 macaroni is better than 2 cents for 3 macaroni because in the 5th term I had 15¢ for 25 macaronis and in the fifth term Rebecca had 10¢ for 15 macaroni. Although we had the same cents at one point, I would get ten more macaroni for 5 more cents; that is why I think 3¢ for 5 macaroni is better than 2¢ for three macaroni.

These give some insight into the kind of thinking these students are doing about the problem.

SOME POSSIBILITIES FOR ASSESSMENT

Two ideas are central to this module. First, a rate establishes a constant relationship between two quantities. Second, equivalent rates follow patterns in their relationship to the base rate.

There are many assessment opportunities embedded in this module. Close observation of a group or an individual can reveal a great deal about their thinking. As you observe, ask yourself: Can this student build a rate series? Does she use a model as a referent? Can she explain what a term in the series means? Finding the answers may be less important in the long run than finding good methods and asking good questions, and close observation can help you find those students who have good methods but may not be finding answers easily.

If you decide to question one student or a group of students more closely, ask questions like: "How would you explain that to a student who hadn't learned about it yet?" "Tell me what you're thinking about as you work." "How do you know that you're right?" "What does this number stand for?" It's important not to bombard students with questions yet to probe their understandings so that you can see how they are using this model to support their reasoning.

Student writing and drawing will give an excellent opportunity for you to determine the quality of their reasoning about problems. This kind of work, whether generating problems for others to do or explaining their solutions to each other, allows them to wrestle with terminology, sequence, and logic as they try to capture their thinking on paper. You may want to select pieces of writing to include in their mathematics portfolios.

Asking a student or a group to find one or two strategies for finding best buys will also reveal a great deal about their thinking. You may find this a good assessment of problem-solving strategies and flexibility. Can the students find alternative methods? Do they have ways of beginning these problems? How would they explain their strategies to other students who hadn't learned about rates yet?

These embedded assessment opportunities allow an informal, ongoing assessment of your students' thinking. Keeping records of your observations and copies of your students' work will allow you to reflect on your students' thinking and their methods, and provides the basis for you to make some comparisons among methods.

WORKSHEET 2.1

Generating a series with materials and numbers

Materials (and   )

Rates (use numbers)

WORKSHEET 2.2

Which One's Better?

Janey sells M&Ms out of her giant bag at 4 for 5¢. The machine at the corner store sells you 9 for 25¢. Which is the better deal for you?

Sandy sells New Kids on the Block cards at 10 for 35¢. Is that a better deal for you than Shaun selling them at 12 for 40¢?

Acme sells sparklers for parades. They charge 19¢ apiece. Ace sells them, too, but charges 85¢ for four. Which is the better deal?

How can you tell?

Frosted Flakes has 11 grams of sugar in each 1 ounce serving. Raisin Bran has 13 grams of sugar in each 1 and 4/10 ounce serving. Which one has less sugar for an ounce of cereal?

How can you tell?

Talk with your group to decide whether there is much of a difference and write your conclusions here.

WORKSHEET 2.3

Find-A-Term

The third member of the series based on $\dfrac{1}{2}$ is:

$$\dfrac{1}{2}, \quad \dfrac{2}{4}, \quad \boxed{\dfrac{3}{6}}$$

Find the specified member for each rate series:

What is the fifth member of the series based on $\dfrac{4}{5}$?

How did you do it?

Find the sixth term in the series based on $\dfrac{2}{3}$.

Find the fourth term in the series based on $\dfrac{5}{3}$.

Predict the tenth term in the series based on $\dfrac{7}{20}$.

Try these predictions:

$$\dfrac{4}{5} = \dfrac{12}{?} \qquad\qquad \dfrac{3}{7} = \dfrac{15}{?}$$

Module 3: Sharing cookies

MODULE OVERVIEW

WHAT HAPPENS

Students use fractions and mixed numbers as they solve sharing problems. At first, they work on one-step problems; for example: If 4 cookies are shared equally among 6 people, how many does each person get? If 20 cookies are shared equally among 6 people, how many does each person get? Later, they work on two-step problems, which require them to add fractions. Students are encouraged to refer to their previous work with the area representations they used in Module 1 to help them visualize relationships among different fractions as they develop strategies for adding fractions.

In the final part of the module, students write their own "ridiculous sharing stories" in which a problem in adding fractions is embedded. Throughout the module, they write about and illustrate their solutions.

The activities take about five class sessions of about 45 minutes each. We have divided the activities into sessions. But feel free to alter this division to fit the pace of your class.

WHAT TO PLAN AHEAD OF TIME

❑ Solve the problems for Sessions 1, 2, and 3 yourself. Try illustrating them with the circles, square, and counting materials so that you can become familiar with the kinds of solutions students may invent.

❑ Provide copies of the page of circles (Worksheet 3.1) and copies of the page of squares (Worksheet 3.2). Students should have a plentiful supply (Sessions 1–3).

❑ Provide collections of things for counting such as plastic chips, beans, centimeter cubes, or paper clips (Session 2).

❑ Some teachers like to bring in something real, such as peanuts, to share in Session 2. Bring something small so that each student will get several if they are divided equally (Session 2).

❑ Provide scissors and either scotch tape or glue sticks. Some students prefer to illustrate their solutions by cutting out the "cookies" or "brownies" and attaching them to their paper (optional: Sessions 1 and 3).

❑ Provide copies of Worksheet 3.3, brownie problems (Session 3).

❑ Provide materials students will need to write and illustrate their story problems— paper, rulers, copies of the circles and squares worksheets if they need them, crayons or markers (Sessions 4 and 5).

IMPORTANT MATHEMATICAL IDEAS

Fraction equivalents. Students continue to develop familiarity with common equivalents; for example, the relationship between eighths and fourths, between sixths and thirds, and so forth. Students should begin to "see" automatically that 2/8 of something is the same amount as 1/4 of the same thing and that 4/6 of something is the same as 2/3. Students need continued experiences in different contexts to strengthen and extend their understanding.

Fractions are related to division. Students solve problems that are similar to division problems they have encountered. In these problems, the whole is a number of things rather than a single thing, and the fractional part of this whole is a group of things as well (for example, 1/3 of 60 is 20). These situations provide the opportunity for students to consider how all fractions are related to division.

Adding fractions. Students develop strategies for adding fractions. Although students at this age level may already know the steps in finding common denominators and adding fractions, they may have little understanding of the problems which they can solve in this way. For example, many fifth graders cannot solve the problem 3/8 + 1/4 mentally. They are able to tediously find the common denominator and then add the fractions but cannot reason confidently about how to combine 3/8 and 1/4. In this module, students develop their own strategies for adding familiar fractions and continue to construct mental images which help them visualize the relationships among these fractions.

Finding common denominators. Although procedures for finding common denominators are not taught explicitly in this module, many of the strategies students use involve finding common denominators. By referring to their work in the earlier modules, and by creating illustrations for their solutions in this module, students internalize key relationships which lay the groundwork for intelligent use of common denominators. For example, students learn to visualize the relationships between fourths and eighths and between fifths and tenths. As they combine fractions, they use common denominators in their solutions.

Justifying and explaining solutions. Through writing about and illustrating their solutions, students clarify their own reasoning and find images which help the students visualize fractions.

SESSION 1 ACTIVITIES

Introducing the problem: Sharing cookies

Introduce the following problem to the class by drawing 7 circles on the board:

If you had 7 cookies to divide up among 4 people, how could you do it?

Encourage students to discuss how they would start and what they would do next. Illustrate their ideas on the board. For example, if a student says, "I'd start by cutting all the cookies in half," divide your circles in half. After a solution is reached, ask students how much each person would get. Accept different ways of naming a person's share: 1 + 1/2 + 1/4 or 7/4, for example.

After one solution has been found, ask for alternative strategies for approaching the problem as well as alternative ways of recording the solution. For example, alternatives might include the following:

❏ Give everyone one cookie and then divide the rest of the cookies in half; give everyone a half; then divide the last cookie into quarters and give everyone a quarter. Each share is 1 + 1/2 + 1/4.

❏ Divide all the cookies into quarters; give each person one of the quarters from each cookie. Each share is 7/4.

❏ Give everyone one cookie; then there are three cookies left; cut a quarter out of each of these cookies and put them together; now there are four 3/4 of a cookie. Each share is 1 + 3/4.

Do one more example with the whole class, encouraging alternative solutions. Try, for example, 11 cookies divided among 8 people. You might want to use squares instead of circles this time to give students a different model. Even changing the shape of the "cookie" can change the problem. For example, students may more readily see how to divide a square into fourths, whereas they might find a circle easier to divide into fifths. By shifting models, students learn to cope with new contexts and build up a repertoire of strategies with which they are comfortable.

Throughout this discussion, encourage students to prove that their approach works by illustrating it or applying what they know about the relationships of fractional parts.

Small group work on cookie-sharing problems

Students work in pairs or threes, using the pages of circles and pages of squares provided (Worksheets 3.1 and 3.2).

Provide these two problems to the groups:

❏ Share 4 cookies among 6 people.

❏ Share 8 cookies among 5 people.

Their task is to divide the cookies among the people evenly and to decide how many cookies each person got.

At this level, many students will know the algorithms for finding these answers. However, their task is not to provide just the answer but to use the circles or squares to show a proof of their solution. The group can help each other figure out the solution, but each student then draws and writes about the solution, including how much each person's share was (see the TEACHER NOTE: Are these problems too easy for fifth graders?). For fifth graders, a "proof" is simply a convincing argument. First, students convince themselves that they have an approach which works. Then, through writing, drawing, and talking, they communicate their solution and convince others.

For example, students' written solutions for the first problem, illustrated with appropriate pictures, might be:

❏ I divided all four cookies in half. Then each person got 1/2, and that used up 3 of the cookies. I divided the last cookies into sixths, so each person got 1/6 more of a cookie. So each person got 1/2 + 1/6 of a cookie.

❏ I divided all the cookies in six parts. So there were 4 x 6 = 24 pieces altogether. So each person could get 4 pieces, so each person got 4/6.

Note that these responses are not in "lowest terms". At this point, allow students to express their solutions in any way, as long as they can show how their solution works. Don't insist that they combine or reduce the fractions. In the discussion of these problems at the beginning of Session 2, students can decide which of their solutions are the same as they compare their solutions.

Some students will be content with dividing the circles and squares by drawing lines to show the parts. However, some students feel that they need to cut out the whole shapes, cut them into fractions, and physically divide them up before they are sure of their solution. Other students cut out the shapes and fold them to figure out fractional parts. If possible, provide scissors and scotch tape or glue sticks so that students can choose the method which works best for them. Teachers have found that it is a good idea to discourage the use of markers or colored pencils during Sessions 1 and 3. In these sessions, coloring seems to be a distraction rather than an aid.

It is easy to create more problems for groups who need additional challenges:

❏ Share 7 cookies among 8 people.

❏ Share 3 cookies among 9 people.

However, teachers who have used these activities recommend investigating each problem thoroughly, exhausting all possibilities, before moving on to new problems. Students need to solve the problems themselves, articulate their solutions, compare their approaches with other students' strategies, and try to understand solutions which are different from their own. As you observe students at work, keep track of students' mathematical confusions and insights and of alternative strategies invented by the students to help you choose a problem for the discussion at the beginning of the next session.

Module 3: Sharing cookies

TEACHER NOTE: ARE THESE PROBLEMS TOO EASY FOR FIFTH GRADERS?

The Sharing Cookies problems may at first seem to you like they are easy problems for fifth graders. However, students in classrooms who used these materials found some of these problems quite difficult when they had to illustrate and prove their solutions. Although many of these students knew the procedures for adding fractions and for reducing fractions to lowest terms, they did not know how to reason about fraction relationships. Without the rote procedures they had memorized, they were unable to estimate or to add simple fractions. For example, in one group, students had figured out that a person in one of the cookie problems would get 3/8 and 1/4 of a cookie. "So," asked the teacher, "how much is that altogether?" After a long pause, one of the students said, "That's what's hard to figure!" Other students in the same class had trouble adding 1/2 and 1/8.

In the second session, a summary discussion of students' answers, especially to the second problem, is critical. In one end-of-the-year fifth-grade class, solutions to sharing 8 cookies among 5 people included 2/3, 4/6, 25/32, 3/4, and 5/12. As students explained their strategies and illustrated them, other students grappled with their own understandings, reevaluated their own strategies, gained new insights, and learned approaches which they were able to apply in later sessions. The goal of this discussion is not to identify a single, "right" method for all students to adopt but to expose students to a variety of ways to think about the problems.

8 cookies 5 people.

Each person gets 1 and $\frac{6}{10}$.

$\downarrow$

Give each person 1 cookie
Then split each one in hafe →give each on person
then split ito $\frac{1}{10}$ s and Give each person $\frac{1}{10}$ = $\frac{h}{4}$ fe

1 and $\frac{6}{10}$.

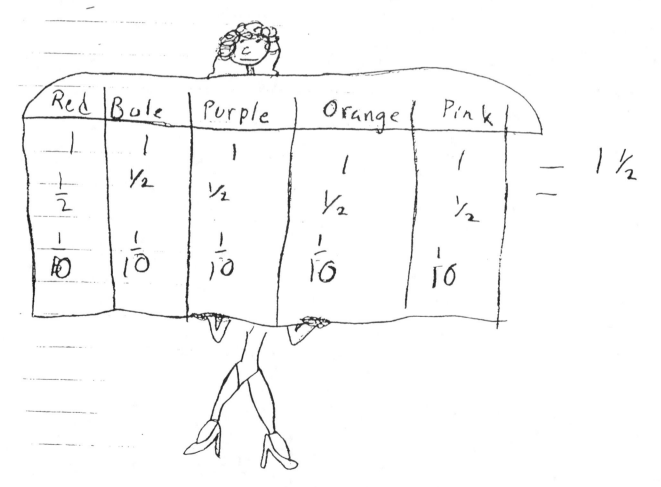

Red	Bule	Purple	Orange	Pink	
1	1	1	1	1	— 1½
$\frac{1}{2}$	½	½	½	½	—
$\frac{1}{10}$	$\frac{1}{10}$	$\frac{1}{10}$	$\frac{1}{10}$	$\frac{1}{10}$	

Figure 3.1

8 cookies
5 people   Rebecca   & Anika

First we gave each of the
five people one whole cookie. Then
with the remaining three cookies, we
divided each of them into fifths. Then
each person got 3/5 of the remaining
three cookies. So, each of the five
people got 1 3/5 of a cookie.

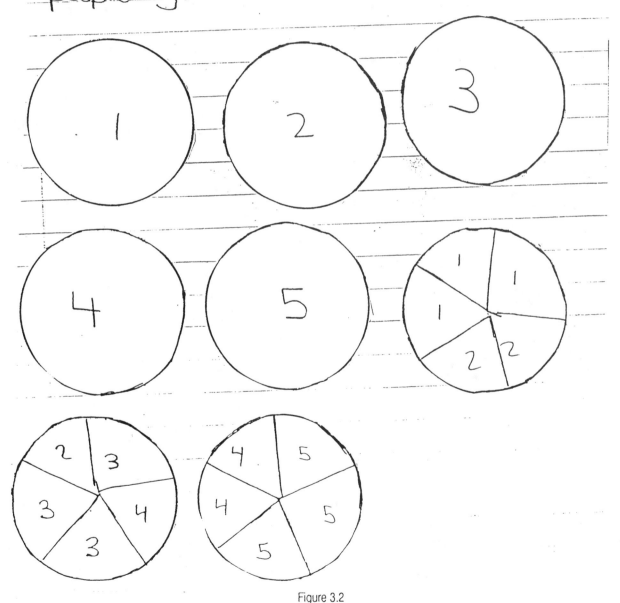

Figure 3.2

6 people 5 brownies

cut the 5 brownine
① in half.

② give a half to everyone.

③ cut the two brownies into 1/12

④ give 1/12 of the brownies to
the people.

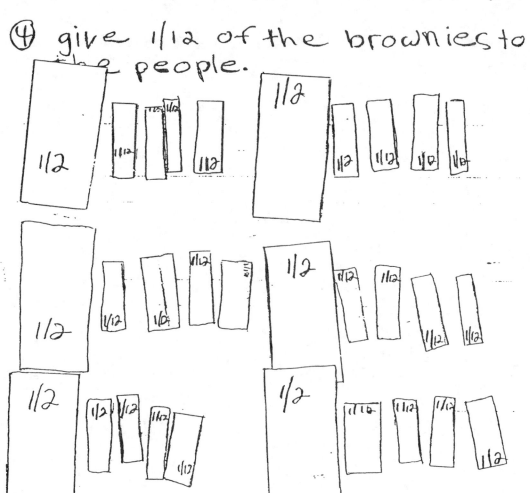

Note: The rectangles used in this and subsequent illustrations to represent the fractional parts were cut out of square "brownies" (Worksheet 3.2) by students and then pasted onto their solution pages.

Figure 3.3

Module 3: Sharing cookies

SESSION 2 ACTIVITIES

Discussion: Comparing strategies

Choose one of the problems from the students' work in small groups in
Session 1 for a whole class discussion. Allow time for a variety of students
to explain and illustrate their approaches to solving the problem.
Encourage other students to ask questions when they do not understand a
student's method. If there are different answers, which is highly likely, list
all the solutions on the board. Why are there different answers? Are some
of these answers actually the same? How can you show that is true? (See
the DIALOGUE BOX: 8 Cookies and 5 People, for an excerpt from such a
discussion.)

What if it's not cookies?

A final question, which has promoted vigorous discussion in some classes,
requires students to think beyond the cookie-sharing situation to other
problems involving the same fractions. Use one of the problems students
have already done; for example:

**You decided that if you share 7 cookies among 4 people, each person will
always get 1 and 3/4 cookies. If you divide 7 things in 4 equal portions, will
each portion always be 1 and 3/4? What if there is a relay race that is 7 miles
long and there are 4 runners on a team? How far does each person have to run
before he or she hands off to the next? Is the problem the same as or different
from the cookies problem? Why? What if you have seven gallons of gasoline to
divide up among 4 cars?**

Remember, in discussions like these, your role is to ask students to
explain and illustrate their thinking, encourage students to ask each other
questions, and keep track of alternative theories. Telling students what is
right will not help them develop important mathematical ideas that they
can really use. Let students know that their thinking is important, that the
process of struggling with a problem is what mathematics is about, and
that answers are not always arrived at the first time a problem is tried.

A different kind of problem: Many more cookies (or whatever) than people

**Before we leave the cookies, I want you to try another kind of problem. Find a
solution, but I 'd also like you to see whether you think this problem is
different from the ones you did in the last session.**

If you have actually brought cookies or peanuts or some other item which
is to be shared, bring it out now and let students know how many there are
to share (or assign a small group of students to count them). Otherwise,
you can pose the problem in hypothetical terms: "If I brought a bag of
peanuts which contained 150 peanuts, and I wanted to share them
evenly... ." The following discussion is based on a class of 26 students in
which the teacher brought a bag of 150 peanuts.

**In some of the fractions problems we've been doing, you are trying to find a
fraction. In this case I think I know what fraction I want. I want each of us to**

get 1/26 of the peanuts. Do you agree? Why do I say a fair share is 1/26 of the peanuts?

After some discussion, ask students to estimate the number of peanuts in 1/26 (choose the appropriate fraction for your class) of the peanuts; that is, a fair share for each student. How can you tell about what fraction of all the peanuts that would be? If some students suggest calculating, acknowledge that would give them the exact answer; but point out that you are first trying to figure out a reasonable estimate.

Now I'd like you to work together to figure out as exactly as you can how many peanuts would be in a 1/26 share. I want you to use the materials to prove your solution.

Students work on this problem in pairs for a few minutes, using the beans, chips, or other counters you have provided. You can also provide one or two other problems of this kind, for example:

❏ Find 1/30 of 105 cookies to show how many cookies each of 30 people can have.

❏ Find 1/10 of 85 peanuts so that 10 people can share the peanuts equally.

When most groups seem to have a solution, provide some time for students to share their approaches. Through working on these problems, students will probably notice the similarity between fractions and division. If they do not point out this relationship, you can use their solutions as the basis for asking them about it ("that looks like the same way you might demonstrate a division problem"). See the DIALOGUE BOX, It's Just Like Dividing, for an excerpt from such a discussion.

Extension

Here is a more difficult problem which some students may enjoy working on:

Carlo and Elena bought a bag of 75 peanuts to share between themselves and their friend Alma at the baseball game. Alma said she had just had lunch and that she didn't want too many peanuts, so they decided that Carlo and Elena would each have twice as many as Alma. What fraction of the peanuts did each of them have?

DIALOGUE BOX: 8 COOKIES AND 5 PEOPLE

[The teacher draws 8 circles and 5 stick people on the chalkboard.]

So what did you do first?

Jean: Give each person 1 cookie.

What should I do to the picture?

Jean: Take one cookie and draw it next to each of the people; that's 5; then erase the 5 from the pile.

[The teacher draws one circle next to each of the stick people and erases 5 of the original 8 circles.]

Kano: Now split the 3 cookies in half, and you're gonna be left with a half remaining.

Tell me what I should do to the picture.

Kano: Split the 3 cookies in half. [Teacher does so.] Now each person gets a half, and you've got one half left. [Teacher draws a half circle next to each stick figure and erases all but a half of one of the original circles.]

Tanya: Now divide it into fifths.

How?

Tanya: Well I was thinking of a square.

OK. We can try it with squares, but let's see if we can solve it with the circles first. Can anyone follow up on Tanya's idea?

Ricardo: Yeah, split that half into fifths.

Tanya: Yeah, one-fifth.

Exactly what do you want me to do here?

Sam: Split the half into five parts as equal as you can make them. [Teacher does so, following Sam's directions.]

Alice: And give one of the pieces to each of the people. [Teacher does so.]

OK, so what have I got?

Chris: A whole and a half and a fifth.

What about Chris's idea?

Other students: Yes...no...one and a half and a fifth...it's not a fifth, though.

There's some disagreement about what this little piece is. Can someone explain the confusion?

Anna: It's like a fifth of the half.

Josie: Yeah, it's not a fifth of the whole cookie.

How can you tell?

[Josie comes up and draws a square cookie, splits the cookie in half horizontally, and then splits one of the halves into five parts.]

What can you say about Josie's picture?

Ricardo: It would be ten...a tenth. Because if you did the same thing with the other half, there would be ten pieces.

So now what does each person have?

Jimmy: One and a half and a tenth.

Cary: One and six-tenths.

Ellen: One and three-fifths.

Are those all the same? How do you know?

Ellen: Because you take the six-tenths and divide it by 2, and it's three-fifths.

But someone explain to me about the six-tenths.

Maria: It's like the picture Josie did. There's five-tenths in the half and then one more.

Ellen: And you divide by 2 and it's three-fifths.

So Ellen is claiming that three-fifths and six-tenths are the same. Can anyone prove it?

Phoebe: You can split a fifth into two tenths, so you have one for every two.

You have one for every two?

Phoebe: Yeah, a fifth is twice as big, so, see, you have six-tenths, so two of them make a fifth, and two of them make another fifth, and the last two make a fifth. Two, two, and two make three-fifths.

I wonder if anyone could show me how that would work on Josie's picture.

[later...]

Does anyone have another way?

Carla: Once you have the 3 cookies left, you divide each of the cookies into five parts.

Jonathan: Yeah, that's how I was thinking about it. You give 3 pieces to each person.

Carla: So you have one and three-fifths.

...

DIALOGUE BOX: IT'S JUST LIKE DIVIDING

[In this class, students have been working with round plastic chips and beans to count with.]

Josie: We made 26 piles and we gave out the chips, one by one to each of the stacks. So we got 5 chips in each stack. So everyone can have 5, and there's 20 peanuts left over.

Cary: Yeah, and we couldn't cut up the chips, but we figured everyone could at least have a half a peanut more, because that would only take 13 peanuts, and we still had 20.

Karen: We decided you couldn't give out the leftovers. It's not like with cookies. It's silly to divide up half a peanut.

Cary: No, it isn't. Because most of the peanuts are double. So you could find at least 13 out of the leftovers that are double peanuts, and people could split them up.

So what did you think 1/26 of the peanuts would be?

Josie: 5 and 1/2 and a little bit.

OK, so how did you and Alma do it, Karen?

Karen: Well, we knew it was going to be about 5 because of our estimate.

Explain about your estimate.

Alma: It was like what Sara said when we talked about it before. There's six twenty-fives in 150, so you know six people could get 25, but you have to give everyone 26...

You have to give everyone 26 peanuts?

Alma: No, it's the other way. I mean, you have to give peanuts to 26 people, not 25.

Karen: So you can't give them 6. That would be too much.

Alma: Yeah, so we made 5 piles with 26 beans in each, and then we only had 20 left, so we knew we didn't have enough to give everyone one more. So it's five.

So let me see if I understand. Josie and Cary made 26 piles with 5 chips in each pile, like this [draws a few groups of five on the board], and Karen and Alma started with 5 big piles with 26 in a pile, like this [draws one big group of 26 circles on the board]. Did anyone do it differently?

Students: We did it like Karen... we did it like Josie...

These two ways look pretty different to me. Do they both work?

Jonathan: I like Josie's way, because it's like the way you'd really do it. It's 26 people and you're giving out 5 peanuts to each one, so it's not piles of 26, it's piles of 5.

Jean: Yeah, but we figured it out Karen's way and we liked it better because we didn't have to make lots of tiny little piles.

Jimmy: It's really the same. In Josie and Cary's, each person gets a pile, but the way we did it— it was like Karen's— each person gets one from each pile.

Maria: Yeah, it's like dividing. If you divide 5 into 10, it's 2, and if you divide 2 into 10, it's 5. Either way, you figure it out.

Are fractions like dividing?

Sam: Sure, like here, it's just the same.

How is it the same?

Sam: Well, you just divide it out either way.

You divide it out?

Sam: Each person gets the same amount.

So you divide up the peanuts evenly. Where's the fraction, though?

Anna: It's the leftover part of the peanuts. You have to divide them up into smaller parts, like halves.

But I thought Sam was saying something about that giving everyone a fair share was like fractions. What can anyone say about that?

Kano: It's parts. That's what fractions are, even parts.

Chris: And so is dividing something up. Like 5 into 10, you get two fives.

And how could that be a fraction?

Chris: Cause 5 is half of 10.

...

SESSION 3 ACTIVITIES

Introducing the problem: Brownies and more brownies

As you did in Session 1, introduce the following problem to the whole class. Write only the first part (1) on the board first (or read it aloud and record key information on the board). Discuss alternate approaches with students. Then present part (2). Discuss with students their solutions to part (2) and then to the final question (3), requiring them to add their two solutions.

1. I invited 8 people to a party (including me), and I had 12 brownies. How much did each person get if everyone got a fair share? (How can you prove your answer?)

2. Later my mother got home with 9 more brownies. We can always eat more brownies, so we shared these out equally too. This time how much brownie did each person get?

3. How much brownie did each person eat altogether?

How could you show what happened here? How can you be sure? How could you demonstrate that your solution works? (See the TEACHER NOTE: Strategies for adding fractions.)

Small group work: Brownie problems

Students work in pairs or threes, using the pages of squares to work on the 2-part brownie problems provided on Worksheet 3.3. The problems are:

1. I invited 8 people to a party (including me), and I had only 3 brownies. How much did each person get if everyone got a fair share? We were still really hungry, and I finally found 2 more brownies in the bottom of the cookie jar. They were kind of stale, but we ate them anyway. This time how much brownie did each person get? How much brownie had each person eaten altogether?

2. Six crows found 4 brownies that had fallen out of somebody's picnic lunch. These were very suspicious crows, and they made sure that no crow got any more brownie than any other crow. How much did each crow get if everyone got a fair share? Later one of the crows found 3 more brownies that had fallen in a ditch. She tried to fly away with them herself, but the other crows saw her, so of course they all had to have their fair share. This time how much brownie did each crow get? How much brownie had each crow eaten altogether?

3. I invited 6 people to lunch (including me). Esmerelda brought 5 brownies. We were really tired of brownies by now, and we were glad that Esmerelda hadn't even brought one brownie for everyone, but we had to be polite and eat them. We divided them out evenly because no one wanted to eat more than they had to. How much did each person get if everyone got a fair share? Then, Alvin invited us all over to dinner, and guess what there was for dessert? Brownies! We were still being polite, so we ate them. Unfortunately, this time there were 8 brownies for the 6 of us. This time how much brownie did each person get? How much brownie had each person eaten altogether?

Their task is, again, not to provide just the answer but to use the squares (or circles) to show a proof of their solutions. Each pair or group of three must come to a consensus about a solution. Then they collaboratively write about how they solved each problem, including how much each person's share was altogether, and use appropriate illustrations to prove the solution.

For the final part of each problem, they must come up with a single fraction or mixed number, although it need not be in lowest terms. That is, an acceptable solution is 4/6 or 2/3 but not 1/2 + 1/6.

Although three problems are provided, two problems may be enough for most groups.

TEACHER NOTE: STRATEGIES FOR ADDING FRACTIONS

In this session, students move from solutions such as "1/2 and 1/8" to combining these fractions into a single fraction. It is likely that many students will want to use rote procedures they have learned to add these two fractions. If students show you a solution such as,

$$\frac{1}{8} + \frac{1}{2} \qquad \frac{1 \times 4}{2 \times 4} = \frac{4}{8} \qquad \frac{1}{8} + \frac{4}{8} = \frac{5}{8}$$

ask them to prove that 1/2 and 1/8 is actually 5/8. They can draw a picture, use the blank squares or circles, or use their geometric designs from Module 1. Some students may have internalized images and relationships about fractions which allow them to reason about these additions without explicitly using models. Here are a couple of students' solutions:

❑ I can tell that 1/2 and 1/8 is 5/8 because first I took a square and split it in half. Then divide each half in four pieces and you can see that there are eight pieces in the whole thing. So there's four in a half, and if you color in one more, that's 5/8.

❑ It's easy to tell because however many pieces there are, half of them are in 1/2. So if it's 8 pieces, 4 of them make 1/2. So 1/2 is the same as 4/8 and another eighth makes 5/8. (If you have sevenths, then it's not so easy because it's an odd number.)

During this module, the emphasis is on combining fractions into a single fraction but not on naming this fraction in any particular way. For example, in one problem, some students might end up with 2/3 as their solution, while others will end up with 4/6. How they name their fraction will usually be related to the strategy they used to solve the problem. Rather than insisting on a "lowest term" answer, encourage students to compare their answers to see which ones are the same and which ones are different. It is more important for students to recognize that 2/3 and 4/6 describe the same total quantity than for them to choose one or the other as more "correct."

Throughout these activities, students work with familiar fractions— halves, thirds, fourths, sixths, eighths, and possibly twelfths. They make use of their experiences in Module 1 to help them visualize ways of combining fractions. However, we do not expect them to be combining fractions which are not related to each other (e.g., 2/7 + 3/4 or 2/3 + 1/4) during this unit. If students get stuck trying to add less familiar fractions, for example, when they are making up their own stories in Sessions 4 and 5, encourage them to give themselves fractions they can work with more easily. The focus of this part of the unit is to familiarize students with those combinations of fractions they should eventually be able to add mentally rather than to teach them general rules for adding all fractions.

Module 3: Sharing cookies

1. 8people (1) 3 brownies

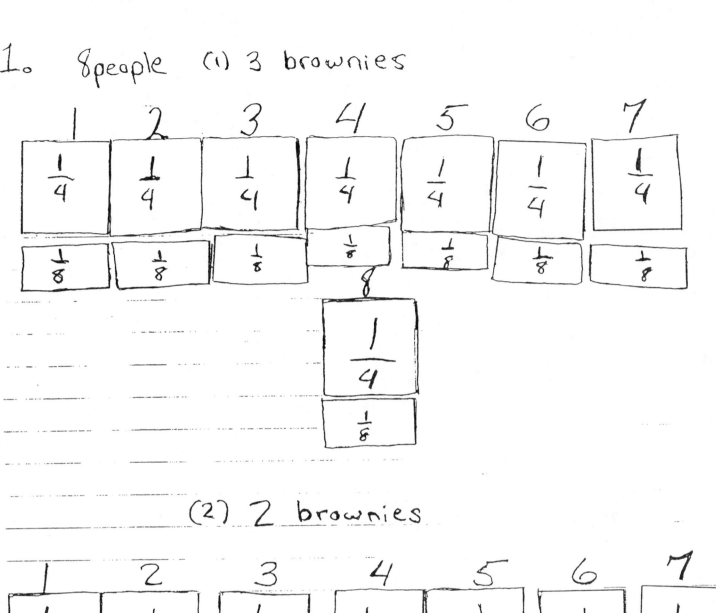

(2) 2 brownies

Each person got $\frac{5}{8}$ of a cookie.

Figure 3.4

① 3 brownies 8 people
cut 2 of the brownies into fourths
give each person 1 forth
cut the brownie that is left into eights
give each person 1 eight
$\frac{1\ 2}{4\ 8}\frac{3}{1}\frac{1}{8}=\frac{3}{8}$
each person gets $\frac{3}{8}$

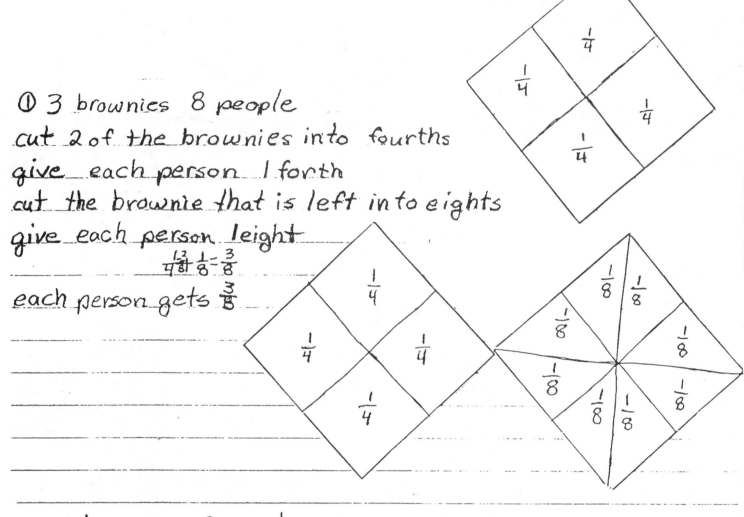

2 brownies 8 people
cut each brownie into fourths
give each person 1 fourth
each person gets 1 fourth $=\frac{1}{4}$

each person all together gets 5 eighths $\frac{5}{8}$

$\frac{3}{8}=\frac{3}{8}$
$+\frac{1}{4}=\frac{2}{8}$
$\overline{\phantom{+\frac{1}{4}}\frac{5}{8}}$

Figure 3.5

(1) Each crow gets $\frac{4}{8}$ a brownie.

(2) Each crow gets $\frac{1}{2}$ a brownie.

3) Eac crow got $\frac{7}{6}$ or $1\frac{1}{6}$ a brownie.

6 crows

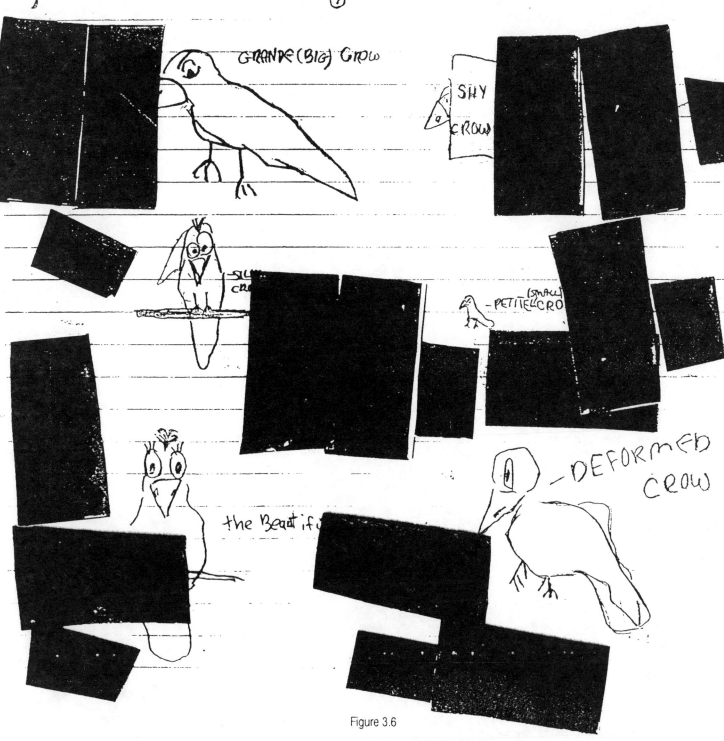

GRANDE (BIG) Crow

SHY CROW

PETITE CROW (SMALL)

the Beatif...

DEFORMED CROW

Figure 3.6

SESSIONS 4 AND 5 ACTIVITIES

Making up ridiculous sharing stories

Students work in pairs or individually to make up a story in which they describe how some group shared something (part A) which required use of fractions and then shared some more of it (part B), again requiring fractions to share evenly. Then they add the two fractions from parts A and B to figure out how much of the something each member of the group ended up with. For instance, here are examples of the kinds of stories which have been written by fifth graders:

Squirrels and Acorns

There were 4 squirrels who brought 6 acorns to their home and split them up evenly. How much did each squirrel get? Later, one of the squirrels found 5 more acorns. How would each squirrel get an equal share of the new acorns? How many acorns did each squirrel get altogether?

The Early Bird

3 birds found 4 worms. They all wanted the same amount of worms. They had finally found 4 worms, so they did not want to lose dinner just because of a small disagreement. So they put their small brains to work, and they came up with a solution. Later, they went out again and found only 2 worms. This was hard to figure, too, but they did. How many did each bird get the first time? How many did each bird get the second time? And so how many worms did each bird eat?

The task is really to make up a ridiculous story, and students can embellish the context to make it more of a real story. Fantasy is encouraged! However, while the problem embedded in the story can be challenging, the students who create the story must also be able to solve the problem and illustrate their solution.

Their task includes:

❑ writing the story

❑ drawing a picture of the story situation (optional)

❑ drawing a picture or diagram to illustrate their solution (including figuring out what fractional part of the something was in each share and then in the total)

❑ writing an explanation of their solution.

Students should make some rough drafts of their problem and its solution, then make a final "publishable" version of story and illustrations. Examples of fifth graders' stories are attached. You may want to read one or two of these to the class for inspiration.

You might want to have students complete their problems in one extended session. Some students have created elaborate stories and pictures which they have needed two class sessions to complete.

If students create situations in which they construct fractions which they cannot visualize and combine except by using memorized procedures, help them find numbers to use in their stories which will result in familiar fractions (halves, thirds, fourths, sixths, eighths, and possibly twelfths).

Make sure you leave time for students to read their stories to the rest of the class or for students to try each other's problems.

Extension

One class used this activity as a chance to share different languages spoken by the students in the class. Students had a chance to see each others' stories written in English, Spanish, Armenian, Korean, Thai, and Tagalog, among others.

Tina's Story

Lavon and I got 10 cakes and shared them with Alison, Rochell, Betsaida, Moonie, Kevin, and Michael B. How many cakes did each person get if they all got equal amounts including Lavon and I?

$$(1\frac{1}{4})$$

Then Marisa came and brought 20 more cakes and left them for us to eat. How many did each person get now?

$$(2\frac{2}{4})$$

How much cake did each person get in all?

$$(3\frac{3}{4})$$

$$
\begin{array}{c|c}
1 & \frac{1}{4} \\[2mm]
2 & \frac{2}{4} \\[2mm]
\hline
3 & \frac{3}{4}
\end{array}
$$

Below is the diagram Tina used to illustrate her solution:

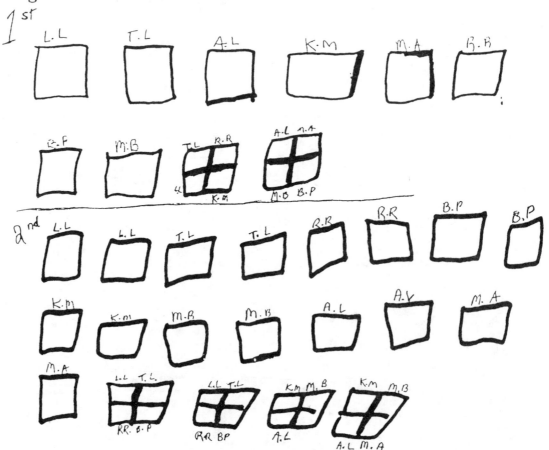

Module 3: Sharing cookies

Althea's Story

An alien from planet KX2 came to earth and found what he called "sweet mush" (we call it sponge cake). Now on this alien's planet the creatures loved cake. So when he flew back he had 25 "sweet mushes" in his flying ship. Unfortunately he had to share these cakes among 40 aliens. How much sponge cake did each alien get?

Another alien from planet KX2 came to earth and was fortunate to get 100 sweet mushes. How much sponge cake did each of the forty aliens get this time?

How much sponge cake did each alien get in all?

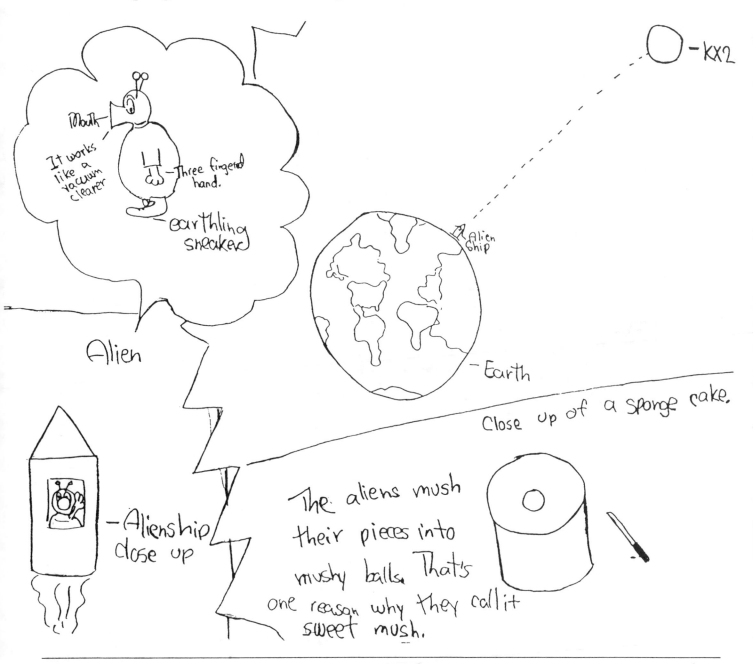

Close up of a sponge cake.

The aliens mush their pieces into mushy balls. That's one reason why they call it sweet mush.

Althea's Solution

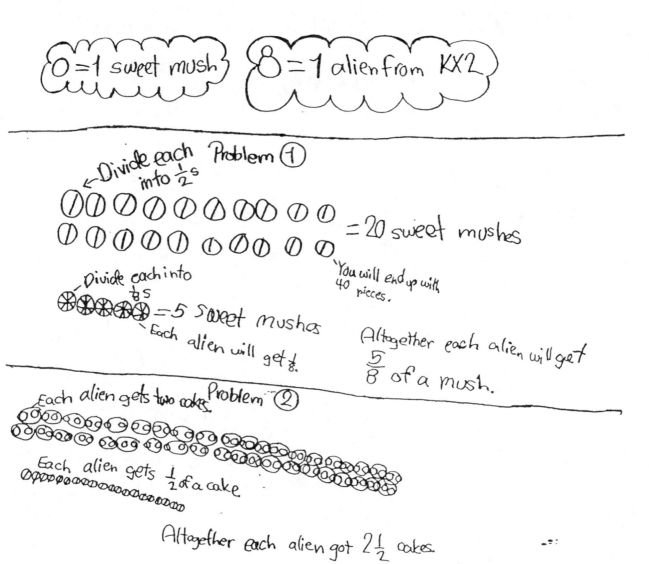

O = 1 sweet mush   8 = 1 alien from KX2

←Divide each into ½s   Problem ①

= 20 sweet mushes

You will end up with 40 pieces.

Divide each into 8s

= 5 sweet mushes

Each alien will get ⅛.

Altogether each alien will get $\frac{5}{8}$ of a mush.

Each alien gets two cakes.   Problem ②

Each alien gets ½ of a cake.

Altogether each alien got $2\frac{1}{2}$ cakes.

Maura's Story

I was absolutely bored stiff. There was nothing to do. Suddenly, an idea hit me! I could have a party! I rushed to my fridge. I found a six pack of sodas. I put them on the table and searched more. Nothing good enough.

The party was a last minute thing so when I called Janine, Tom, Ronda, Simon, Susie, Ronald, Mary, Joey, Randy, Susan, Laura, and Sam, I wasn't surprised when Sam and Ronald couldn't come. Oh well! Well everyone else turned up. I counted everyone. Including me, there were 10. Where was Ronda? Just then, she pranced in happily with 2 more sodas.

"Hi!" she said to me.

"Hi!"

"I brought these."

"Thanks!"

"Knowing you, I was sure you wouldn't have enough!"

"Yeah. Gee, thanks."

How much did each person get?

Maura's Solution

I poured the soda into 8 cups. "Hmmmmmmmm!" I thought, "I could divide 6 cups in 1/2, give each person 1/2, and have 2 1/2 left over. Divide the 2 wholes into 1/11's and give each person 1/11 from each. Then I could divide the remaining 1/2 into 1/11's. Let's see, 1/2 of 1/11 is 1/22 so give each person 1/22. That totals 8/11 of a bottle each."

SOME POSSIBILITIES FOR ASSESSMENT

In this module, students use a sharing model as they continue to develop their notion of fractions as equal parts of a unit. They explore the relationship of fractions to division, and they solve and construct problems in which different fractions are combined. There are many opportunities for assessment embedded in the module activities. In particular, you might save examples of students' writing— both their solutions of problems you give them and the problems they create themselves in the last two sessions.

An additional type of problem for assessing student understanding is a "reverse sharing story," such as this one:

Clara's brother baked cookies for her and 7 friends she had invited over for her birthday. After they shared all the cookies evenly, each of the eight people at the party had 1 and 3/4 of a cookie. How many cookies were there to begin with? Illustrate your solution with a picture or diagram.

A problem like this can also be worded this way:

Five friends shared out some brownies evenly. Each person got one whole brownie, a half a brownie, and a sixth of a brownie. How many brownies did they start with?

In these problems, students have to think about the fractional parts in relation to a whole which they must construct, and they need to consider different size parts in relation to the same whole.

WORKSHEET 3.1

WORKSHEET 3.2

WORKSHEET 3.3

Brownie Problems

1. I invited 8 people to a party (including me), and I had only 3 brownies. How much did each person get if everyone got a fair share? We were still really hungry, and I finally found 2 more brownies in the bottom of the cookie jar. They were kind of stale, but we ate them anyway. This time how much brownie did each person get? How much brownie had each person eaten altogether?

2. Six crows found 4 brownies that had fallen out of somebody's picnic lunch. These were very suspicious crows, and they made sure that no crow got any more brownie than any other crow. How much did each crow get if everyone got a fair share? Later one of the crows found 3 more brownies that had fallen in a ditch. She tried to fly away with them herself, but the other crows saw her, so of course they all had to have their fair share. This time how much brownie did each crow get? How much brownie had each crow eaten altogether?

3. I invited 6 people to lunch (including me). Esmerelda brought 5 brownies. We were really tired of brownies by now, and we were glad that Esmerelda hadn't even brought one brownie for everyone, but we had to be polite and eat them. We divided them out evenly because no one wanted to eat more than they had to. How much did each person get if everyone got a fair share? Then, Alvin invited us all over to dinner, and guess what there was for dessert? Brownies! We were still being polite, so we ate them. Unfortunately, this time there were 8 brownies for the 6 of us. This time how much brownie did each person get? How much brownie had each person eaten altogether?

Module 4: Making and using fraction strips

MODULE OVERVIEW

WHAT HAPPENS

Students work out relationships among fractions on a linear measurement model, using a nonstandard unit of measure. Linear measurement provides a context in which the need to consider and use fractions occurs naturally. Throughout this module, students use paper strips to measure lengths and fractional parts of lengths. Students begin by estimating lengths of some object in the room in whole number and fractional parts of a paper strip. In a second activity, students work in small groups to find objects which are different fractions of the strip in length. In both these activities, students generate ways of subdividing a strip into familiar fractions: halves, thirds, fourths. In Session 2 they partition the strips (like rulers) using their own invented methods, and compare their strategies with one another. In Session 3, the students are given an array which has halves, thirds, fourths, and sixths correctly marked on it. They complete other parts of the array by using spatial patterns and their strips. Finally, in Sessions 4 and 5, the students use the strip-rulers in playing games which require them to order fractions and to estimate fractional lengths in terms of the strips. We have suggested one way to break the unit into 5 sessions; but feel free to adjust the timing as works best for your class.

WHAT TO PLAN AHEAD OF TIME

❑ Photocopy enough of the pages of strips (Worksheets 4.2–4.6) to provide one page for each group. It is best if you photocopy each worksheet on a different color of paper. Then photocopy on white paper about twenty copies of the sheet of unspecified strips (Worksheet 4.1) to use in the first class and to keep as backup for students who use up their strips or would like to make additional strips. Cut up two pages of these unspecified strips to use in the first class. Think of a way students can store their strips so they don't get lost between sessions (Sessions 1–4).

❑ Pick a piece of furniture for students to estimate the length of (in strips) that is not exactly a multiple of the lengths of the strips. The strips are 8 and 1/2 inches long, the width of a regular sheet of paper. Students will need to measure the object you choose themselves, so it is best if it is something replicated in several places in the room, perhaps a standard size desk or table or a piece of easel paper (Session 1).

❑ Try making the strip rulers and array yourself. If possible, work with another person so that you can discuss your strategies. Read the

TEACHER NOTE: Children's strategies for partitioning strips (Session 1).

❑ Make a collection within reach of each group which includes: a few scissors, a ruler, felt pens or colored pencils or crayons in 4–5 different colors, and some of one kind of smaller object of standard size such as paper clips, centimeter cubes, or inch cubes (Sessions 1–5).

❑ Plan a way to divide your students into groups of two or three students who work well together (Sessions 1–5).

❑ Photocopy the fraction arrays worksheets (Worksheets 4.7–4.8), one for each student and quite a few extras of 4.7. Because photocopying changes the lengths of lines, be sure you use the original worksheet every time you copy. If you have an overhead available, make a transparency of the completed array, Worksheet 4.8 (Session 3).

❑ For each group, provide two pieces of large newsprint paper (18 inches by 24 inches or larger), a set of marked strips (Worksheet 4.11) photocopied on card, and sets of fraction cards (Worksheets 4.9–4.10) photocopied on card (Sessions 4–5).

IMPORTANT MATHEMATICAL IDEAS

Understanding what is meant by partitioning a whole length into equal fractional lengths. In the Geometry and Sharing Cookies modules, students partitioned area into equal parts. Here they will partition length into equal parts.

Using mixed numbers. As in the Sharing Cookies module, some of the activities will involve using fractional numbers larger than one whole. Linear measurement allows students to see fractions arrayed along a number line as measures between units.

Learning to use a measurement model in which the fraction represents a distance from a starting point. In the area model, each section can be separated from the others so that, for example, the whole can be cut into separate thirds and each one labeled "1/3." However, in the measurement model, which is a number line, the labels denote the distance from the left end (or zero point) of the measuring strip (ruler) so that the labels are different from one another and in order of increasing size (e.g., 1/3, 2/3, 3/3).

Understanding that 2/n, 3/n, 4/n, etc. are built by iterating 1/n. Students may refer to "two 1/3s" or "1/3 and 1/3" rather than "2/3". Here they will have experience building fractions from the unit fraction, seeing, for example, that 2/3, 3/3, 4/3 are made from repetitions of 1/3.

Comparing fractions in an array. Students use the arrays to find equivalents and to compare fraction size by finding patterns.

Estimating fractional lengths. A central activity throughout this unit is generating and sharing strategies for making estimations based on visual images. Given a unit of length, the students are asked to estimate how long a certain fraction of that length would be. The length of the strip is kept constant to allow students to develop mental images of individual fractions and to allow for comparison of fractions. In the next module, students will be involved in the more complex process of comparing fractions of different sized units.

SESSION 1 ACTIVITIES

Estimating length in strips and fractions of strips

Before you begin, put the scissors, pens, rulers, and assorted objects out for each group of students.

While the students watch, lay one strip along the table, or desk, or piece of easel paper or whatever object you have selected for students to estimate. Ask the students to estimate how many strips will fit along the whole length. Write all of the estimates on the board and allow students to change their minds when they see each other's estimates. After generating a list of estimates, encourage a few students to explain the thinking behind their estimations. What is going on in their minds when they estimate in strips and fractions of strips? How do they think about this process? (See the DIALOGUE BOX: Estimating lengths.)

After a few students have explained their thinking about the overall measure, lay out strips. When less than one more whole strip is needed, ask students to estimate what fraction of a whole strip the remaining length is.

We have three strips and some part left over. What fraction of a strip do you think the leftover part is?

Write the students' estimates on the board for consideration later. Accept all responses in the form the students give them. For example, write "one sixth and one sixth" as 1/6 +1/6 or "half of a sixth" as

$$\frac{\frac{1}{2}}{6}$$

Sometimes another student disagrees. If a disagreement occurs, do not erase the answer until the student who suggested it decides to remove it. We have found that students often correct their own answers when they see them written or when they hear other students' responses. Also, do not simplify answers unless the students suggest it. (Write both 1/2 and 2/4 on the board if students give those answers.) If one student simplifies another's answer, write both versions.

Inventing ways to measure with an unmarked strip

After making estimates, students work in their groups to measure what fraction of a strip the remaining piece is. Hand out pages of unmarked strips (Worksheet 4.1) for students to cut apart and share. If it is inconvenient for each group to measure the object, also give them a strip with the length of the fractional part of the measure marked on it. Tell them you will be interested in hearing how they went about measuring and what fractional answers they figured it to be. They may use any of the objects you have put on the tables, including the rulers, but their measures are to be in fractions of a strip.

After a few minutes, when all the students have tried something and many have begun to suggest answers, gather students together to talk about and demonstrate what they did. List all the suggested measures on the board and allow the students some time to compare these measures to the estimates they made earlier.

How did your estimates compare with the measurements you made when you could work closely with the strips?

What did you do to find the fraction of a strip more exactly?

The purpose here is to share the ideas they have generated about how to find fractions of a strip. Ask students to explain and to demonstrate what they did to measure the piece of the strip. If most students suggest folding, ask students who found fractions without folding to demonstrate what they did. If everyone used folding, ask them to think how they might find the fractional part without folding.

An issue may come up about what is the exact answer. Try in these activities to measure carefully, but the main idea is to develop strategies for figuring out fractional lengths and to practice making estimates of lengths. Ask the students to compare the answers they did get.

Are any answers very close to each other?

Are there any answers which look different but really are the same?

Fraction length scavenger hunt

In this activity, students look for things in their work area (they might use body parts as well) which measure different fractions of a strip in length. The idea is for them to pair many different fractions of a strip with objects which have those lengths. Each group will generate its own list of fractions and objects.

Students make a list of the things they measure and their measures. As a challenge, you might suggest they rewrite the lists to put things in order by length. You may find that students tend to find only unit fractions (those with a numerator of 1, such as 1/2 or 1/3). By probing and posing questions, encourage them to find other fractional lengths as well.

Suggest a few fractional lengths to find and collect a few other ideas from the students.

Can you find something which is 1 and 1/2 strips in length?

Can you find something which is a third of a strip in length? two thirds of a strip?

What fraction of a strip is your hand span?

Circulate around the room and observe the strategies the students are using. If a student suggests she found an object of a certain measurement, ask her how she knows.

Before the end of class, bring the students together to share and illustrate all the different lengths of things they found. Suggest they compare some of the things which they think have the same length.

DIALOGUE BOX: ESTIMATING LENGTHS

How many strips do you think it will take to measure the length of the table?

Holly: Three.

Seth: Maybe three and a half.

Curran: Four.

Nicole: Three and three-fourths.

Sara: Three and three-fifths.

Zach: Three and an eighth.

Alex: Three and two-fourths.

Tanya: That's three and a half.

Alex: (laughing) I know!

Tanya: Oh, three and four-eighths...and three and eight-sixteenths.

I'd like to hear the reasoning behind your estimates.

Seth: I just set it in my hand (holding thumb and forefinger as calipers) and it seemed like a little more than three.

Rea: When you put it on the table, I took it in my head and put one on, so it was a little less than three and a half.

Holly: It just looked like three. I just thought of that size in my head and put it on the table.

Jason: I thought three plus a little tiny bit more.

Zach: I knew it was just a little more and I estimated it was about one eighth. It just looked like it.

Who said four? Can you explain that?

Curran: When you put it on, I thought three plus one more time.

Nicole: I don't think it's four but I think it's more than three and a half so I think it's three and three-fourths.

In this discussion, the teacher wanted the students to become aware of the mental images they use to estimate and the common sense knowledge of fractions they have developed.

SESSION 2 ACTIVITIES

Mental images

Tell students they will be making a set of rulers so they can measure lengths in fractions of the strips. Show a regular ruler and point out that they will be making small marks like those on the ruler along the top edge of strips:

This ▭ not this ▭

Figure 4.1

Draw a rectangle the shape of a strip on the board and ask the students to close their eyes and imagine it as a ruler which can measure halves. Where would the mark for halfway across be? After enough time for students to imagine the measuring strip, ask a volunteer to come up and put a mark on it half way across the top edge. Draw another blank strip and give time for students to imagine it marked for measuring thirds. Ask another volunteer to mark where one third of the way and two thirds of the way across the strip would be.

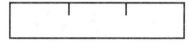

Figure 4.2

Making fraction rulers and discussing strategies

For each fraction ruler, students follow this sequence:

1. While sitting in a group with one or two other students, each student works alone to mark a strip.

2. In order to come to a consensus about the placement of the marks, students explain to each other how they figured out where to place them. If the members of the group all used the same method, they try to think of another method they could use to check the placement of the marks.

3. When students are in agreement within their group, they compare with someone in a nearby group.

Hand out the page of halves strips (Worksheet 4.2) to be cut out and marked in halves. Save the other templates until students have made the halves rulers, checked them with one another, and discussed the strategies they used. Students will complete their halves strips quickly.

Note: The focus of this task is on partitioning the strips to place marks. We have found that some children become quite confused when they also try to label the marks with numbers. For a further discussion of this, see the TEACHER NOTE: Labeling strips and arrays with numbers. The blanks for making measuring strips are marked "HALVES", "THIRDS", etc. so that the children will not need to write the numbers.

If there are groups with no child who strives for equal portions, you will need to engage the group in conversation about the confusion between social knowledge in which "halves" can be different sizes and mathematical knowledge that the parts need to be equal. You might tell a story about one child taking the "larger half" of the cake and leaving the "smaller half" for another child. Is that fair? What does half mean? Is there such a thing as a larger half?

Suggest that when they finish, students throw away extra bits of paper and place their halves rulers out in front of them so you will know they are ready to go on. Pass out the page of thirds strips (Worksheet 4.3). If you think they can handle it, hand out the page of fourths strips (Worksheet

4.4) at the same time, but keep in mind that thirds are more difficult for most students than halves. You may want to wait to give students the fourths strips until they have finished thirds. We suggest that you not point out relationships between halves and fourths at this time. (See the TEACHER NOTE: Encouraging children to develop their own strip-making procedures.)

At the beginning of this activity, wander among the groups to be sure each group understands the goal of making an accurately marked set of measuring strips. After that, you can become a researcher, observing the strategies students are using and probing their understanding. See examples of questions in the DIALOGUE BOX: Strategies for thirds and fourths. For some approaches your students may use, see the TEACHER NOTE: Children's strategies for partitioning strips. Encourage interaction within pairs and threes to be sure that all children are involved in the decision of how to mark the strips. Suggest to students who finish early that they write about how they figured out where to place marks for halves, thirds, and fourths.

Discussion of strategies

When the students have finished fourths and perhaps done some writing about their strategies, stop the work and bring students together to explain and show the ways they partitioned thirds and fourths. Ask students if they can tell you about a way they learned from someone else in their group or a way they worked out together.

You might make fifths (Worksheet 4.5) or skip them for now. Some groups have enjoyed the challenge, others have found that making too many different strip-rulers can be tedious. Students will have another chance to do fifths and other denominators in Session 3 when they work with an array.

Before continuing the strips work, discuss with the students how they can use what they have already done to mark rulers in sixths. Do not tell them yourself but encourage students to think about what they might do, and see what strategies they come up with.

How can you use the strategies you developed to make halves and thirds and fourths to help you make the sixths strip?

How can you use the strip rulers you already have?

Again, when the students get back to work, they discuss their strategies and compare markings with their partners and then with another group nearby. Hand out pages for sixths strips (Worksheet 4.6). Challenge them to come up with several different ways the sixths can be made. Students then work together to write about several possible strategies. Each student might write about a different way. Students who finish early can write as well about their methods of making halves, thirds, and fourths measuring strips. A set of these writings could be put together by each group. Students may later add instructions for additional strips if they wish.

When everyone seems ready, call the class together for another discussion. Ask students to explain and demonstrate how they made rulers for sixths. This discussion is a good time to ask what other measuring strips can be made by using strips they have made (eighths and twelfths, and tenths if any students have made fifths). Finally, have students go back and find the actual measure of the object the whole class estimated in Session 1 (if they haven't already).

DIALOGUE BOX: STRATEGIES FOR THIRDS AND FOURTHS

Some student ideas for partitioning into thirds have included:

"I put something straight like a pencil where I thought one third was, and then I put something else for two thirds."

"I took my finger and measured a third and then put another and another; and if it was too long, I made it a bit shorter; and if it was too short, I made it a bit longer and tried again."

How do you check if all portions are equal?

"I folded over."

How would you know if they weren't equal?

"A little piece would stick out."

"I compared with Derek's."

What if you were working alone? How could you check?

"I would measure one part and be sure the other parts were the same."

Here are some things students have said about fourths:

"We made marks exactly in the middle, and then we made marks in the middle of those parts."

How did you find the exact middle? Did you fold?

"No, I put sticks down and measured with my fingers."

"I folded it in half and then took the edges and folded into where the groove was."

DIALOGUE BOX: STRATEGIES FOR SIXTHS

To start out with, does anyone want to say how they got sixths?

Inge: What I did was I just got thirds and then divided it into sixths.

So you folded it into thirds?

Inge: Yeah.

Did you use the thirds strip?

Inge: No.

Why did you start with thirds?

Inge: I don't know, I just did.

Jason: What I did was I folded it in half, then folded it into three on one side and three on the other side.

Why did you do it that way?

Jason: Well, three and three is six.

James: I took thirds, then folded it into sixths.

You did it like Inge. Why did you start with thirds?

James: Well, if you took where half of each third was, it's a sixth.

Andy: Six is a multiple of three.

Anything else about sixths? Did anyone picture in their mind 3 pieces?

Zach: That's about what I did for most of 'em. I folded it in half, then folded each part until I got eighths.

Good. That's making a connection. How did you go about doing eighths?

Holly: I took my fourths and marked it; then I folded it in half.

TEACHER NOTE: LABELING STRIPS AND ARRAYS WITH NUMBERS

In these activities, students use the strips for measuring length. If they choose to label them, they should put the labels in the way they are on rulers. We have found that some fifth-grade students think of the strips as a part-whole area model for fractions, not the linear measurement model which we intend here. They draw lines all the way from top to bottom of the strip as if slicing a strip of cake into pieces. They may label the parts correctly for their area model this way:

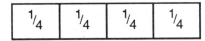

Figure 4.3

or mix models and label incorrectly this way:

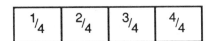

Figure 4.4

In either case, they will probably have difficulty using their strips as a ruler. With the labels *in* the sections, they are not sure whether to measure to the middle of the section or to the left or right edge of the section. Thus in this work we encourage students to make the marks on the strips small and just near the top edge as on a ruler, and to wait to write fraction labels until they have done the arrays.

Later, in labeling the array, they should put the numbers in order as on a number line and attach the numbers to the marks, not put them in the spaces:

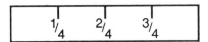

Figure 4.5

TEACHER NOTE: ENCOURAGING CHILDREN TO DEVELOP THEIR OWN STRIP-MAKING PROCEDURES

When we first tried this activity, we asked students to mark the strips in an order which reflected relationships between denominators; we encouraged them to use halves in making fourths and thirds in making sixths. We found that students who did not already know about these relationships tended to mimic the teacher without understanding. We came to believe that the students need to figure out these relationships for themselves. So now we ask the students to make the strips in order of increasing denominator. They can use the strip-rulers they have already completed to help them make others, but we do not tell them how to do that. Your students will bring some knowledge of relationships among halves, fourths, and eighths and among thirds, sixths, and twelfths from the Geometry module. By working together and describing their methods of placing marks, they will learn strategies from one another.

TEACHER NOTE: CHILDREN'S STRATEGIES FOR PARTITIONING STRIPS

Although adults would be likely to fold strips to partition them, we have found it best to let students decide for themselves how to do this task. One group of fifth graders in a trial class never folded at all. They placed pencils and Cuisenaire rods along the strips until the spaces between them looked equal and then marked under the pencils.

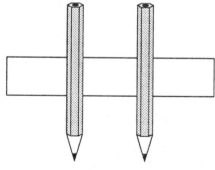

Figure 4.6

This group paid more attention than most fifth graders to the layout of the portions across the whole strip. To make such a strategy possible, we suggest you make available to the students an assortment of rulers, sticks, and small objects.

How the students approach this task depends on the knowledge of fractions they bring to it. Here are some approaches your students might use:

Folding randomly

Some children will bring little knowledge of fractions to the task. They will think only that they must get a certain number of parts. They may just fold over and over and open up and count the parts. They will be satisfied with four parts for fourths, not caring if the parts are equal. If they fold into more parts than they are aiming for or if it is pointed out that one part is too long, they might tear off a bit, not maintaining the original length of the whole.

More shares, smaller shares

Other children will notice that as the denominators increase, the unit fraction becomes smaller; for example, that one-fifth is a bit smaller than one-fourth. These students will estimate the length of one-fifth and then fold to copy that length across the strip or iterate that length using their thumb and forefinger as calipers. If they get the number of portions they expected they may not survey the whole strip to see if the last portion is smaller or larger than the others. They assume that because they used a good strategy, the portions must be equal.

Seeing the whole strip

Children who keep the strip out flat and place markers at equal intervals along it are likely to do a more accurate job than either of the first two groups. They will look at the whole strip to be sure there are the desired number of equal portions. Some will arrange cubes or paper clips so that the pattern is the same in each portion. For example:

These children often create mental images of the place of individual fractions in the whole, remembering for instance that there are 2 and 1/2 fifths on each side of the halfway mark.

Using equivalents

Finally, some children will use equivalents to help them. Most commonly, this occurs in getting fourths from halves and eighths from fourths. Children can be encouraged to think of how to use the strip rulers they have already made to make sixths and when they work with the array in Session 3, they may use this strategy to find eighths, tenths, and twelfths.

Each time we have done this activity, we see the difficulty children have grasping even the most basic concepts about fractions. Even after completing the Geometry and Cookie modules, some children will require probing from peers or from the teacher to realize that the whole must be maintained and the portions be equal. However, without these concepts, further work with fractions can have little meaning.

SESSION 3 ACTIVITIES

Completing the array

Tell students they will be making a fractions chart, like the one sometimes found on classroom walls, which shows many fractions together. Pass out a copy of the partially made fractions array (Worksheet 4.7) to each student.

We have found it helpful to introduce the arrays by suggesting that a creature is walking across each of the lines. It stops to rest at the marks. The students may like to suggest a different creature for each line. Encourage using the marks on one line to place marks on another, either through using equivalents or looking at spatial patterns.

An ant takes a rest halfway across the line. Its resting spot is labeled on the halves line.

If an ant walks across the fourths line and stops halfway, where will that be?

What other lines have a mark at the ant's halfway stopping point?

Demonstrate how to hold a cardboard strip vertically next to the half mark to show which other marks are lined up right under the half.

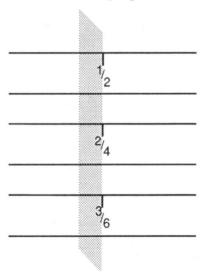

Figure 4.7

What are the fraction names of these marks?

What fraction should we write at the mark halfway across the fourths line?

How can you tell which other lines will have marks for stopping places exactly halfway across?

Which lines will not have any mark halfway across?

What would the label be for a mark halfway across the twelfths line?

Take suggestions until you have all the labels for one half. Have the students label those marks on their charts. For information on some of the issues which may arise about labeling the arrays, look again at the

TEACHER NOTE: Labeling Strips and Arrays with Numbers, following Session 2.

Now you may proceed in different ways. You may want to continue leading this discussion to look for equivalents to 1/3; or you may think it better for students to work together without your guidance to figure out how to continue marking and labeling their arrays.

You may plan for the class how much of the array to complete or give students the option of doing as much as they can. Some students may want to fill in the whole array. Options for continuing the work with the array include the following:

1. Label the lines already marked and do the placement and labeling of the marks for fifths.

2. Do number 1 and then find and label all fractions on the eighths, ninths, tenths, and twelfths lines which have equivalents to the marks already placed.

3. In addition to 1 and 2, do the sevenths, ninths, and elevenths by estimating their places in the "arches" or "rainbow" pattern of the array.

As you observe the students working, look for and probe errors which seem to represent a misconception. For example, we have seen fifth graders put a fraction in every row in the half column so that 3/7 is under the half. When we point out that the intervals on the sevenths line don't seem equal, the students eventually work out the inconsistency. You do not need to stress accuracy for its own sake although some students will challenge themselves to be perfectly accurate.

When they have done as much as they can, give them a completed array (Worksheet 4.8). Give them a little time to check their array against the printed one.

Put up the overhead array for the students to brainstorm the patterns they see. To start this, you might ask what clues they used to help them place additional marks on the array. Then continue to elicit observations about the general patterns on the array.

As an extension, some classes have made a large array on a wall or floor in their own classroom or in a public place where other classes can see it.

SESSIONS 4 AND 5 ACTIVITIES

Using fraction strips: Activities and games for visualizing and comparing

Students play two kinds of games: Island Hopping, which requires visual imagery of lengths, and Capture Fractions, which allows for using any models to compare fraction size. Students first do some activities to prepare for the games: the Estimating Lengths activity prepares students for the Island Hopping game, and the Finding Equivalents and Which Is More? activities prepare them for the Capture Fractions game. You may decide what order you think best to present these activities and games. Island Hopping can take a session or longer if students become interested in designing challenging game boards to play on.

1. Preliminary activities

Estimating lengths:

1. With all of the arrays and strips turned upside down in front of them, one student in a team names a fraction and everybody estimates with their hands apart the length that would be in terms of a strip. These can be parts of a strip, for example 3/4, or they can be mixed numbers, for example 2 and 1/3 strips. The student who named the fraction then turns the array over or assembles strips together so that the other students can check their estimates.

2. A student names an object smaller than one strip in length (such as a paper clip, pencils of different lengths, a finger, hand-span, a book width, etc.). Each student estimates the length of the object in parts of strips and then the student who named it measures it.

Finding Equivalents: Students work together to compare fractions of different denominators on the arrays to make lists of fractions which are equal to each other. What fraction on the array has the most names?

Which is More? Working in teams with their arrays in front of them, one student closes her eyes and, holding thumb and forefinger apart like calipers diagonally, touches her array in two places (on two different lines) while the others are not looking. She names the two fractions nearest to where her fingers land, for example, 3/5 and 7/8. Other students, without looking at their arrays, name the larger fraction or write them in order, as 7/8 > 3/5 and explain their reasoning. Then the leader shows which is actually larger.

Fractions between Fractions: As a more difficult challenge, players try to name a fraction between two fractions picked from the array.

2. Games

Capture Fractions: In this game, commonly called "war," players deal out the whole deck of cards (in this case fraction cards which you or the students make). Worksheets 4.9 and 4.10 provide forty fractions to start with. Players place their cards in a stack face down in front of them. Players all turn over one card at the same time. The player with the highest number exposed wins all of the turned-up cards. If two or more players turn up cards with the same highest value, they each place three more cards face down and one up. The highest of the face-up cards wins the whole bunch. Players explain to each other why they think one fraction is larger than another. If they cannot agree, they may look at their arrays. The game may be played on and on, with players placing winnings under their stacks, or it may be played for one round with winnings put in a separate place and counted when the original stacks are empty.

Island Hopping: This is a game which requires estimating and then drawing fractional lengths. It was designed by a group of middle school teachers and redesigned by fifth and seventh grade students to make it more challenging. Your students may decide to change the rules some more. They may want to draw game boards which require a greater degree of accuracy. Island Hopping has been most successful in classrooms where the students increased the level of difficulty to challenge themselves as they became more familiar with it. It is best played by 2 to 4 students. Students may enjoy playing in teams of two against another one or two teams.

To introduce the game to the students, draw a game board which all students can see. Explain the game and illustrate by actually having two pairs of students play one or two rounds.

❏   The board is a large piece of drawing paper on which the players draw a harbor area in one corner from which to start and three or four islands placed anywhere on the paper (see figure 4.8). Students may wish to name the harbor and their islands. Discourage them from spending too much time decorating their boards. They will need to draw a new board for each game, or they may wish to make copies of their board to try again or to challenge other groups. As they become more expert, they can challenge themselves by making the islands very small or by playing on larger paper.

❏   For playing the game, students will need a set of the marked cardboard strips made from Worksheet 4.11. Students should write the names of the fractions strips on the backs ("Halves," "Thirds," etc.). They may also write labels on the strips and color the backs of the strips in similar colors to those used for their paper strips. The set of cardboard strips is turned upside down nearby. The students can identify the strips by the name (and color) on the back but cannot see the measured marks on the front. Students must pick the length to be used in their turn, for example 11/5, 1 and 3/4, 7/8, before they turn over the strips.

❏   The goal is to start anywhere inside the barrier of the harbor, land anywhere on each island once in any order, and return to the harbor (they are traveling in an amphibious vehicle).

❏   Players take turns. Each uses a different color pen. In a turn, a player estimates the distance to an island from where her last turn finished. She uses the cardboard strips to measure and draw a line of the length she chose. If the line does not reach an island or overshoots it, she draws a line of the length she chose which does not cross any island and "treads water" until her next turn (see figure 4.9). In the student's next turn, she starts from where her line ended in the previous turn. Thus, after a game is completed, the routes of each player can be seen in a different color as a continuous circuit going from the harbor to each island and back to the harbor.

Possible extensions to the Island Hopping game:

❏ Omit halves and fourths from the game to challenge students to use less familiar fractions or have players throw a die each turn to determine a denominator (make dice by marking blank cubes with denominators you would like the students to use).

❏ Suggest that groups of two or three students make up game boards for other groups who will play cooperative solitaire by working together to complete the circuit in the least number of moves.

❏ Make up a game which involves estimating from country to country or city to city on a large world map. You will need a way for students to record their routes without damaging the map, perhaps by using chalk. What distance in miles or kilometers does one strip length represent on the map?

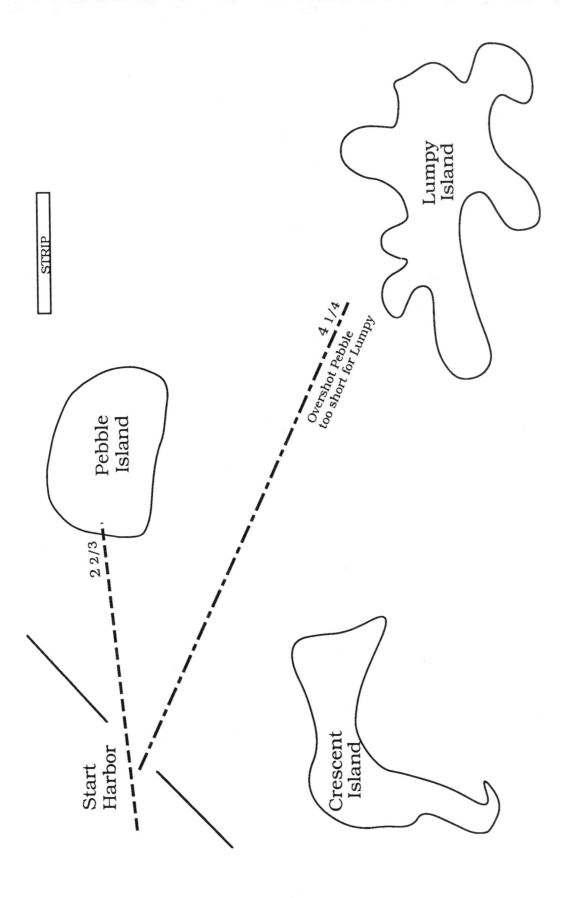

Figure 4.8

SOME POSSIBILITIES
FOR ASSESSMENT

In this module, students have been developing mental images of fractional relationships as they marked their strips and played the Island Hopping game. You can observe students using these skills in the games and activities in Sessions 4 and 5. In addition, we propose two tasks which can be done by the whole class at once or which you can use in individual interviews.

❑ Give students plain paper and have them draw a line across it. Ask them to imagine an ant (or slug or whatever they suggest) stopping for a rest 2/3 of the way across and to mark and label about where they think that would be. Ask them to place other fractions on the same line, perhaps 1/2, 2/5, 5/6, 1/4, and 1/8. This is an estimation task. Accuracy is not expected. It should be done quickly without enough time to fold, etc. You are looking for a general sense of the size and order of the fractions.

❑ Give each student a strip tick-marked in twelfths and have them label the strip with twelfths and with other equivalents.

WORKSHEET 4.1

Extra Strips
Fill in your own label

ut on dotted lines:

WORKSHEET 4.2

Cut on dotted lines:

- -

| Halves |

- -

| Halves |

- -

| Halves |

- -

| Halves |

- -

| Halves |

- -

| Halves |

- -

| Halves |

- -

| Halves |

- -

WORKSHEET 4.3

Cut on dotted lines:

- -

Thirds

- -

Thirds

- -

Thirds

- -

Thirds

- -

Thirds

- -

Thirds

- -

Thirds

- -

Thirds

- -

WORKSHEET 4.4

Cut on dotted lines:

Fourths

Fourths

Fourths

Fourths

Fourths

Fourths

Fourths

Fourths

WORKSHEET 4.5

ut on dotted lines:

| Fifths |

| Fifths |

| Fifths |

| Fifths |

| Fifths |

| Fifths |

| Fifths |

| Fifths |

WORKSHEET 4.6

Cut on dotted lines:
- -

- - - - - - - - - - - - - - - - - | Sixths | -

- - - - - - - - - - - - - - - - - | Sixths | -

- - - - - - - - - - - - - - - - - | Sixths | -

- - - - - - - - - - - - - - - - - | Sixths | -

- - - - - - - - - - - - - - - - - | Sixths | -

- - - - - - - - - - - - - - - - - | Sixths | -

- - - - - - - - - - - - - - - - - | Sixths | -

- - - - - - - - - - - - - - - - - | Sixths | -

Fractions Array

Halves		1/2
Thirds		
Fourths		
Fifths		
Sixths		
Sevenths		
Eighths		
Ninths		
Tenths		
Elevenths		
Twelfths		

WORKSHEET 4.8

Fractions Array

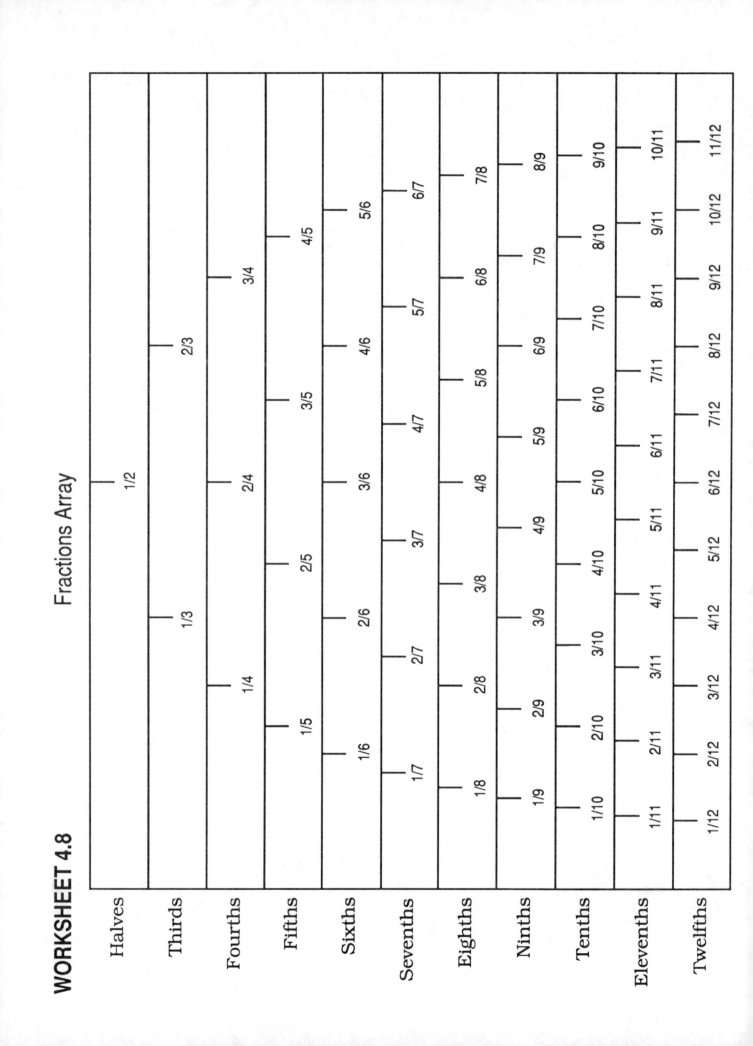

$\dfrac{1}{2}$	$\dfrac{2}{2}$	$\dfrac{3}{2}$	$\dfrac{1}{3}$
$\dfrac{2}{3}$	$\dfrac{3}{3}$	$\dfrac{4}{3}$	$\dfrac{1}{4}$
$\dfrac{2}{4}$	$\dfrac{3}{4}$	$\dfrac{4}{4}$	$\dfrac{6}{4}$
$\dfrac{1}{6}$	$\dfrac{2}{6}$	$\dfrac{3}{6}$	$\dfrac{4}{6}$
$\dfrac{5}{6}$	$\dfrac{6}{6}$	$\dfrac{8}{6}$	$\dfrac{1}{5}$

$\dfrac{2}{5}$	$\dfrac{4}{5}$	$\dfrac{1}{8}$	$\dfrac{2}{8}$
$\dfrac{3}{8}$	$\dfrac{4}{8}$	$\dfrac{6}{8}$	$\dfrac{7}{8}$
$\dfrac{2}{8}$	$\dfrac{3}{9}$	$\dfrac{6}{9}$	$\dfrac{2}{10}$
$\dfrac{4}{10}$	$\dfrac{5}{10}$	$\dfrac{2}{12}$	$\dfrac{3}{12}$
$\dfrac{4}{12}$	$\dfrac{6}{12}$	$\dfrac{8}{12}$	$\dfrac{9}{12}$

WORKSHEET 4.11

Pre-marked
Fraction Rulers

ut on dotted lines:

Halves

Thirds

Fourths

Fifths

Sixths

Eighths

Tenths

Module 5: Using fractions to compare data

MODULE OVERVIEW

WHAT HAPPENS

Students collect data in their own class and use fractions to compare their results with another group or class. To represent these data, they use a model which illustrates discrete data on a paper strip (the "class strip"). Using partitioning techniques developed in Module 4 or by sharing discrete objects, students find familiar fractions that represent the more unwieldy class fractions— such as using 2/3 or 1/2 as good approximations for 19/29 or 16/31.

Initially, class statistics are collected in order to develop ways to find familiar fractions and to make comparisons with data provided in this module. Students then collect data from their class on research questions of their own. Finally, they plan and carry out a survey in which they compare data from two groups (their own class and another class), represent the data in pictures and graphs, and use fractions as one way of comparing the data from the two groups.

The activities take about six class sessions of 45 minutes. This does not include time for collecting data between Sessions 4 and 5. We have indicated a suggested way to break the activities into six sessions, but you may find a better way for your class.

WHAT TO PLAN AHEAD OF TIME

☐ Provide scissors and half-inch, centimeter, or quarter-inch graph paper to make class strips. Also have available the collection of small objects, such as centimeter cubes, which the students used in Module 4 (Sessions 1–4).

☐ Make sure students have their fraction arrays from Module 4 available (all sessions).

☐ Check with your colleagues for good times to collect data from their classes between Sessions 4 and 5.

☐ Duplicate copies of your class list for students to use during their survey work (Sessions 2–4).

☐ Arrange with other teachers the times for your students to collect data in their classrooms (between Sessions 4 and 5).

❑ Provide materials for report and graph making, including crayons, markers, rulers, scissors, graph paper, construction paper, glue, and large sheets of plain paper (Sessions 4–6).

IMPORTANT MATHEMATICAL IDEAS

Finding familiar fractions of a group. Students convert unfamiliar to familiar fractions (13/27 of the class is approximately what familiar fraction?). They may use the strategies they developed from partitioning strips in Module 4 or they may use groups of objects to help them visualize the parts of a group to find a sensible, familiar fraction.

Finding the complement of fractions. Sometimes the complement of a fraction gives clues to finding a familiar fraction more readily than the fraction itself. When students collect data to find the number of classmates who have dogs, the complement shows the part of the class which does not have dogs. While it's difficult to find a familiar fraction for 23/31 of something, finding one for 8/31 may be simpler. And while it may be difficult to find 3/4 of a number, it is usually easy to find 1/4.

Collecting and displaying data. Data collection and analysis make important and common use of fractions. Often data are reported in a fractional form, or as a percentage. Through their own work with data, students develop a sense of what relative proportion of a group is being discussed when data are reported in this way.

Recognizing that fractions are always fractions of something. The larger the whole group, the greater number a certain fractional part will be. Thus a greater number of students does not necessarily mean a greater fraction of the class. In the linear class strip model, the lengths of the fractional parts will change as the length of the total strip changes.

Estimating and comparing fractions. Is 4/6 of the group nearly all of it or only about half of it? Is it more or less than 3/4? Using the techniques they developed to divide strips into simple fractions, students can mark the class strip to see what 3/4 of their number is and how that compares with 4/6. This direct comparison means more to many students than the abstract manipulation of symbols. For more information, see the TEACHER NOTE: Estimating fractions.

Recognizing that fractions can be used in making comparisons when individual values would be misleading. If 60 women prefer vanilla and 60 men prefer vanilla, I might conclude that men and women have an equal preference for vanilla. However, if I knew that 120 women and 80 men were polled, I can now see that only half the women but three-fourths of the men preferred vanilla. Fractions (or percents) provide ratios which can be compared directly.

Writing about mathematics. Students present their findings by writing about their data collection research and illustrating it with diagrams. This written presentation allows students to think through their work, explain it clearly, and present a variety of models for thinking about fractions.

SESSION 1 ACTIVITIES

Introduction: What fraction of the class has a dog for a pet?

In the next few classes you are going to be using fractions to study our class and to compare it with others. You'll collect data and use fractions to describe yourselves first. In later sessions, you'll make up your own questions and collect data to compare our class with another class.

Many times statistics are reported as fractions. For instance, if you wanted to give a picture of how usual it is to own a dog in the United States, you might say a certain fraction of U.S. households have dogs. What fraction of households in this country do you think have a dog for a pet? Half? More than half? What do you guess? Will our class data be about the same as your estimate? Let's see.

Stand near the center of a long wall, perhaps the classroom wall with the blackboard or out in the hall. Ask all students who have dogs to line up on your right and all those who do not to line up on your left. Change your own position as necessary to be the dividing point between the two groups. Check that the students are spaced as evenly as possible. Make a mark or leave an index card taped to the wall where you are standing and mark the beginning and end of the line of students. When the students return to their desks or stand where they can see the wall, ask for their rough estimates of the portion of the whole distance taken up by the dog owners and the portion taken up by the non-owners.

Write down the estimates on the chalkboard. Ask a few students how they figured their estimates. Some may have counted. Others may have estimated the proportion of the distance on each side of the mark. Whatever methods work for them are fine.

Now collect the numerical data. Count and record on the chalkboard. If you get fractions such as 19/27 have dogs, 8/27 do not, so much the better. This is real-life data. It's bound to produce messy fractions.

Is this close to your estimate? How can we tell what these fractions mean? What familiar fractions are they close to? Discuss this in your groups. You can use the cubes or other objects to stand for students or try any other method you can think of.

Give students a few minutes to discuss and work out a familiar fraction for the class data. Then bring them back into discussion to share their findings and their methods.

You might end up with two estimates here that are both reasonably close. If students are able to "prove" both approximations, accept them both.

So what you're saying is that about [2/3 or 3/4] of us have dogs. What fraction of the class doesn't have dogs?

Write on the board: We think [between 2/3 and 3/4] of the class has dogs; [between 1/4 and 1/3] of the class doesn't have dogs.

What you did is how people make sense of fractions that are hard to work with. What if I told you that 4235/6382 of the dentists surveyed preferred Dentoon chewing gum? Would you know if that was half, more, less than half, or closer to three quarters or something else? If you want to fiddle with this one, what would you say was a good approximation for it? It's a very hard fraction. Usually in data collection people approximate fractions and report a more familiar fraction so that other people will know what they're talking about.

Using a class strip to find a familiar fraction

When we looked at the fraction of you who owned dogs, you had several different ways to approximate the fractions. I want to show you one more method that will work (but remember, this is only one way). The important thing is that you have some method of showing how you got your answer.

While the students watch, cut out a strip with one unit of length (one centimeter or half inch or quarter inch, depending on which graph paper you have) for each student in the class. Then count along the strip the number of students who own dogs and mark on the strip to separate the number who have dogs from the number who do not.

I am making a strip with one square to represent each student in this class. We can use this class strip to show how many out of the total of you have dogs, and then we can figure out, as you did when you made fraction measuring strips, what familiar fraction that is close to. I can count on the strip so that I can find out how many we're talking about out of twenty-seven. We can mark the strip at (for instance) 19/27 to represent the dog owners on the left and the people who don't have dogs on the right. Now, what familiar fraction is that? It's not easy to know, is it? In your groups, make a class strip like this and find a way to figure out what familiar fraction this is close to.

The students, working in groups, cut out strips, mark the dog owner data on their strips and partition them to find a familiar fraction.

Bring students into discussion again briefly to share their results.

Did you find that the fractions you estimated earlier were the best fit, or did you find other fractions which were closer?

Now collect some more data for which the students can find familiar fractions.

Make a guess. Will the fraction be about the same for cats? More? Less? What do you think it will be?

Collect guesses and again find the fraction of the class that does have a cat and the complement that does not have a cat. You might like to use the method again of lining the students up against a wall to give them a start at finding a familiar fraction; or perhaps you will just take a count. Ask your students about some other pets.

You will end up with two or more fraction statistics (and their complements) about pet owners on the chalkboard. Students will work in their groups to find familiar fractions for these statistics about cats or other pets. Tell students that they do not have to use class strips. You will be interested in any methods they come up with. Make sure students still have collections of small objects available to them. If a group finds more than one method, so much the better.

For one of these results, perhaps a particularly "messy" fraction, have students write about how they found a familiar fraction close to it.

Module 5: Using fractions to compare data

Sharing ways of finding familiar fractions

Take time to have students report what familiar fractions they found for the pet data and to report how they got those fractions. Encourage them to describe methods they thought up themselves. If the only method reported is the class strip method you illustrated, ask if they can think of another method they could use to check their findings. Are the familiar fractions they found the same as they expected when they just thought about the numbers?

Finally, set aside some time to discuss the pet data:

What do these statistics tell us? What can you say about our results?

TEACHER NOTE: ESTIMATING FRACTIONS

Throughout these sessions, the emphasis is on estimating parts of a group. Students will already know some numerical methods that will give them answers, but they may not have a good sense of the quantities these fractions represent. For example, if 19 out of your 27 students have dogs, some students might say the fraction that represents this proportion is 19/27 ("nineteen twenty-sevenths"). This certainly seems like the right answer, but 19/27 is a fraction that is hard to imagine and hard to use for comparison.

When this happens, you might say something like

Sure, 19/27 is a fraction that tells us what proportion of the students in this class have dogs, but it's not easy to imagine what 19/27 of something is. Usually, when people are reporting data they try to figure out a more familiar fraction, like 1/2 or 1/3 or 3/4 or 4/5, that is the closest to the exact fraction. Usually you can come up with a good estimate that is close enough, that is easier to imagine and easier to compare with other fractions.

Ask students to try to reason about what appropriate familiar fraction is close to 19/27. Use questions such as: Is it bigger or smaller or about the same as a half? How do you know? If it's bigger than a half, is it big enough to call it three quarters? How can you tell? If it's bigger than a half and smaller than three quarters, what could it be? Students can use their fraction arrays from Module 4 to help them solve problems like this one.

Some students will use the class strip method demonstrated in this session to estimate. Others might pick a number of discrete objects such as centimeter cubes to represent the students in the class and use grouping to find the familiar fraction. With this model students can start with a hypothesis such as "I think it's close to 2/3", then group the objects in thirds and see if, in fact, the number is close to 2/3 of the whole. Both of these methods require having a hunch about the size of the fraction. In discussions, elicit from the students how they worked out these hunches. If they say "I just knew" or "it just seems about right", ask them to try to be more convincing about their hunch.

SESSION 2 ACTIVITIES

Introduction to comparing with some other groups

In this session students compare some data from their class with some data collected from other sources and presented as familiar fractions. Then they begin to prepare for comparing their class to classes with different numbers of students.

Yesterday we practiced finding fractions of the whole class. We used class strips and objects and different methods of mental arithmetic.

Today we will start using those methods as we do some statistical research. First, you'll warm up by collecting some data to compare with reports from other groups. Then you will make up some questions of your own and you'll do data collection to answer them. Finally, we'll begin to plan how to do some larger studies.

Present some of the following statistics and write the fraction data for each problem on the chalkboard.

Half of American students who were surveyed watch TV for more than 24 hours each week. How do you compare? Do more of you or fewer of you watch that much TV?

In one fifth grade class in Brookline, Massachusetts, 4/5 of the students prefer the Cosby Show to The Wonder Years, but in a different fifth grade class about half the students prefer The Cosby Show and half prefer The Wonder Years. How do you compare? Are your preferences more like one class or more like the other?

In a fifth grade class in Massachusetts, 1/6 of the students are allowed to stay up later than 9:00 on school nights. How about you? Are most of you expected to be in bed by 9:00?

About 4/5 of Americans have never eaten a bagel. How many of you have eaten a bagel? Can you think of a food that you eat frequently and that many Americans have never eaten?

The fraction of American children who are first born in their family is a little less than 5/12. What fraction of you are firstborn children? middle children? youngest children?

[The TV-watching statistic was obtained through a telephone call to Nielsen in January, 1990. The fifth grade statistics were collected by the students in those classes. The rest of the data were found in *Harper's Index* by L.H. Lapham (New York: Henry Holt, 1987).]

For each problem that you pose, collect the data from the class and write their class fractions on the chalkboard. Students work in small groups to find familiar fractions to represent the fractions from their own class and to compare their own class data with the given data.

Is the fraction of this class that watches more than 24 hours of TV each week more than the national statistic? Less? About the same? How can you prove your assertions?

Bring students together to discuss their findings and/or have them write about one of the problems and describe their method of comparison.

Comparing statistics in classes with different numbers of students

Begin a discussion about comparing data from groups of different sizes. Present several situations to help students think about how they can compare groups of different sizes. Several suggestions for guiding this discussion appear below:

We don't know how many students answered the question about how much TV they watch. We can guess it was a lot more than the number of people in this class. Is it still meaningful to compare our class to these statistics? What do you think about this?

In one fifth grade class from Woodland Hills, California, 17 out of 25 students preferred football to baseball. I wonder how our class compares. Does a larger fraction of you prefer baseball? What do you think? Let's take a poll. How might you compare our results with those of the Woodland Hills class when we don't have the same number of students?

In Parkside School, 93 kids take the bus. In Celia Smith School, 252 kids take the bus. Is it more unusual to take the bus at Parkside or at Celia Smith?

Then reveal the missing information:

At Parkside the student population is 105; at Celia Smith, it is 600. Does this change what you say about the comparison?

In our class 19 out of 27 people own dogs. We found out that is a little over 2/3. What if 19 people of a class of 24 students had dogs. Would that still be near 2/3 or would it be a larger fraction or a smaller one? What do you think?

How would a class strip look for a class with a different number of students? How could you make one for a class with three fewer people than we have? How many students are there in half our class? How many in half a class with three fewer students? with ten more students?

The underlying mathematical issue in this discussion is how a fraction can be used to compare groups of different sizes because it expresses a relationship which can be compared directly.

SESSION 3 ACTIVITIES

Generating questions for data collection

You're going to be conducting your own research for the next three mathematics classes. Today you'll choose questions and try them out in the class, just with us. You'll find out some statistics from doing that, like the ones we have been collecting in the last two sessions. Then you'll collect data from another group and compare to see whether they're like us or different. Finally, you'll report the results of your research.

This is a chance for you to ask each other some questions that are really interesting. Let's brainstorm a list of possible questions and then different groups will choose questions or even invent new ones. Here are some to start you off:

Do you have rules about watching TV on school nights?

Do you get an allowance?

Do you have to do chores?

Do you like to sing?

Where do you go to hang out after school?

Do you have to babysit for your brothers or sisters?

Record the list as your students generate questions. Follow formal brainstorming rules. No comments on each other's questions, no silliness, keep the ideas coming fast. Write as fast as you can while the ideas are really flowing but wait when they slow down; there will be more. You will be looking for questions for which the answers fall into a few categories. This kind of data lends itself to comparison using fractions.

Data collection: Just the facts, ma'am

Each group of students selects a question, takes a copy of the class list, and circulates to collect the data. It's a good idea to have the students write their question on the top of the class list so that they don't forget it or change it during the data collection process. Once the data are collected, ask students to organize the data and draw a picture or diagram to show the results.

Find the fraction

Encourage the use of a variety of representations of the data but keep an eye out for students who do not use a fractional representation at all. If, for instance, your students produce a bar chart (as they are likely to do), ask them to talk with you about the fraction of the whole class that is represented in each category.

Informal reports

What were the results of your study?

Ask students to show their picture or diagram and to report their results to each other orally. You may want to have the class make predictions of what they think the fraction of the class will be for each question before the results are reported so that they can compare the data collection results with their hunches.

Be sure to ask each group how they got their familiar fraction. Did they use the class strip? Did they use another method? Can they describe and explain how they thought about it?

Module 5: Using fractions to compare data

SESSION 4 ACTIVITIES

Extending the study: Refining questions and techniques

Next you'll be looking at these same questions, but you'll compare our results with another class.

Ask whether anyone had trouble with questions. Were there ambiguities? Were any questions unclear? Do they need to add some categories like "I don't know" or "undecided?" The groups or the class may want to flag questions to be reconsidered.

You will collect data from another class in the school and compare their data with our data. Suppose we were going to compare our class to [Ms. Jones'] class. What can we do?

Ask your class to think about how they could get the information, and how they would compare the two sets of data. Remind them that they would be comparing the fractional part of Ms. Jones's class with your class statistic. The number of students in Ms. Jones's class is likely to be different from the number in your class.

Planning the data collection: How will we do it?

When you collect data from the other group you'll survey, what do you need to know? How are we going to record the results? We had class lists for our own data but we might not be able to get them for the other classes.

The critical information will be the total number of students and the number in each of the categories the students have created.

Finally, decide with the class which other class each group will go to in order to collect data.

Who are we going to ask? How are we going to organize ourselves so we don't all go to the same class?

Now, meet in your small groups for a short time to do three things.

1.   **Revise, if you need to, the question you have decided to work on.**

2.   **Write down your revised question. Survey our class again if your question has changed a lot.**

3.   **Plan when and how will you collect these data.**

As you circulate around the room, make sure that each group has a firm grasp on the task for data collection. If they change the main thrust of their question, they will need to circulate another class list to get responses to their new question.

SESSION 5 ACTIVITIES

Talking about the survey

What happened when you collected your data? Did everything go as you expected?

Your students will return with data and with stories about what happened. They may have some very funny stories. It's often helpful to get those stories out of the way before the analysis of the data is even attempted. During this time, listen for ways to refine their data collection techniques for any further studies you want to conduct.

Organizing the survey data

Remember, we want to compare the results for their class with the results for ours. You have two fractions now, [16/27] and [19/31]. How can you tell which is more? If we're considering sixteen twenty-sevenths of our class and nineteen thirty-firsts of theirs, then which is the larger fraction? Do you have ways to solve this?

Write such an example on the board and invite comments from the class and listen to methods. As long as your students' methods are reasonable, encourage a variety of ways of proceeding. Suggest that they find familiar fractions to compare. To do that, they can group discrete objects, one for each student in the class, or they can make a class ruler for the other class the same way they did for their class and find a familiar fraction on it, using their partitioning strategies. If they use either of these methods, they can use their fraction arrays to compare the familiar fractions. Some might decide to use a more direct comparison which does not necessitate finding familiar fractions. To do this, they make another class strip the same size as their own class strip, perhaps out of plain paper, and arrange along it a number of small objects to represent the number of students in the other class.

Remind your class that they will report informally to each other at the end of this working period so that they can see whether their predictions held true and so that they can find out the results for the other classes. At the end of about fifteen to twenty minutes they need to have a familiar fraction for these new data.

Informal reports: The comparisons

As students are ready, have them report briefly about their comparisons and their findings. They need not make elaborate presentations, but they need to be able to answer questions about how they arrived at answers. And they should develop some theories about similarities and differences. Ask questions like, "I wonder why those are such different results." "Do you have some theories about it?" "Why would that have been true of the third graders?" Encourage the whole class to join in generating hypotheses.

Tomorrow, we'll publish the results of our surveys. Each group will write up their question, the results in this class, the comparative results, and their

theories. You will have to illustrate these results with charts and pictures that help make your data very clear to anyone who reads them.

SESSION 6 ACTIVITIES

Publishing the results of the surveys

Now that you've got your results, we're going to publish them. Each group will make a big poster or chart telling what you did. You might want to do this in a number of different ways, but it's important to use this opportunity to educate others through your posters.

What do you have to include in your writeup?

Generate a list with the class of what their reports should include. Stress the audience aspect of this work— they will be educating other students. At the very least they need to include what their question was, who they asked, their raw data, and *at least two ways of showing the data as a fraction.* They should show the comparison of the two results (side by side class strips), more conventional fraction comparisons (pies or rectangles), or groups of objects which have been compared.

Be on the alert for charts and bar graphs which do not help show a comparison. Let's say that nineteen students in one fifth grade have skis and thirteen in another fifth grade have skis. Which class has a higher proportion of students with skis? A total of nineteen students is indeed more than thirteen students. But if the first class has thirty-two students and the second has seventeen students, the nineteen students represent a smaller part of their class than the thirteen represent of their class.

Challenge your students, then, to write down their interpretation of the comparison. It's not enough to say that there is more. It's important to have some explanation as to why that might be true (see the Sample Student Survey Report and the examples of student work at the end of the module).

These final reports can be posted rather than being read again to the group. Often an oral report is much less rich than the thinking and discussion that has gone on within the small group.

SAMPLE STUDENT SURVEY REPORT

We asked our class and Mrs. Foster's class how many students go to bed
before 8 p.m. on school nights, how many go to bed between 8 and 9 p.m.,
and how many go to bed after 9 p.m. Here is what we found out:

	Before 8	8 to 9	After 9
Our class	5	13	6
Mrs. Foster's class	7	11	4

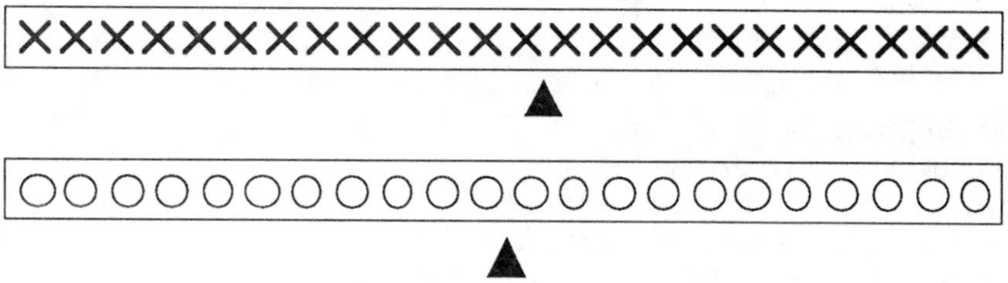

XXXXXXXXXXXXXXXXXXXXXXXX
▲

OOOOOOOOOOOOOOOOOOOOOO
▲

Figure 5.1

We made two strips the same length, but one has 24 kids for our class and
the other one has 22 kids for Mrs. Foster's class. We put marks for
everyone in each class on the strips, and we found out that 1/2 the kids go
to bed between 8 and 9 p.m. in both classes because 12 is half of 24 (our
class) and 13 is really close to 12. And in Mrs. Foster's class we found out
that exactly half the kids go to bed then because 11 is exactly half of 22.
Then we found fractions for the other times by looking at the strips.

	Before 8	8 to 9	After 9
Our class	$\frac{1}{4}$	$\frac{1}{2}$	$\frac{1}{4}$
Mrs. Foster's class	$\frac{1}{3}$	$\frac{1}{2}$	$\frac{1}{5}$

Our conclusion is that about the same fraction of kids goes to bed between
8 and 9 in both classes. But we have fewer kids that go to bed early
because 1/4 is less than 1/3 and more of our class goes to bed late
because 1/4 is more than 1/5.

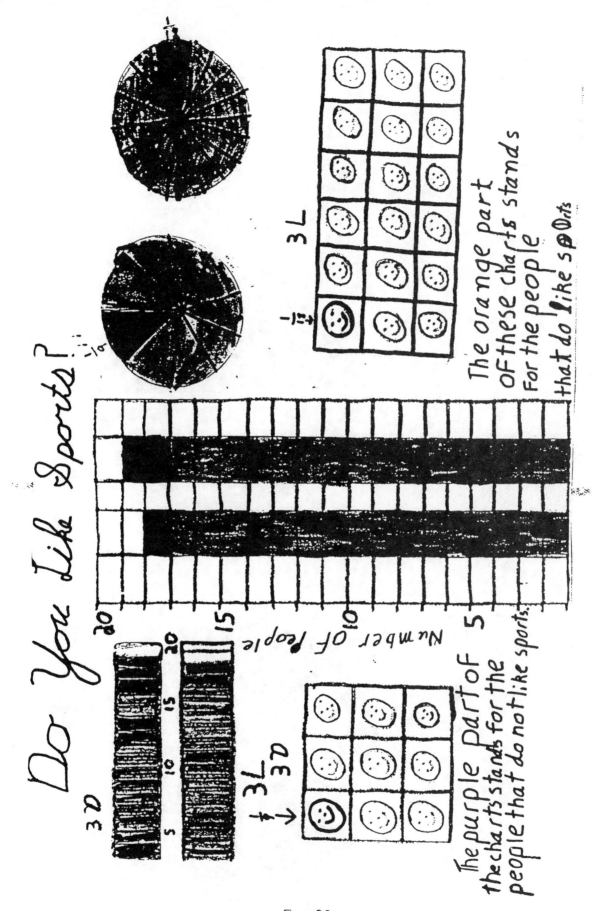

Figure 5.2

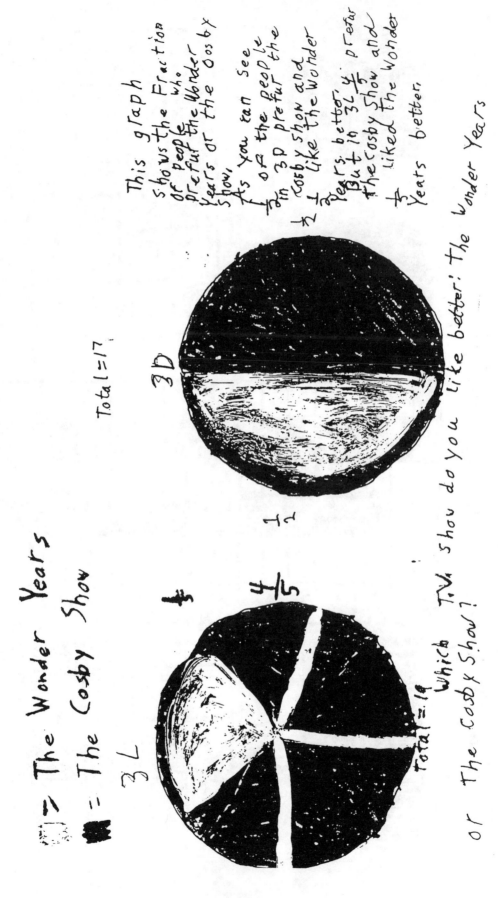

This graph shows the Fraction of people who prefur the Wonder Years or the Cosby Show.

As you can see or the people in 3D prefur the cosby show and like the wonder ½ years better. But in 3L ⅘ prefur the cosby show and liked the wonder Years better.

Total = 17

3D

½

□ = The Wonder Years
■ = The Cosby Show

3L

⅘

Total = 19

Which TV show do you like better? The Wonder Years or the Cosby Show?

Figure 5.3

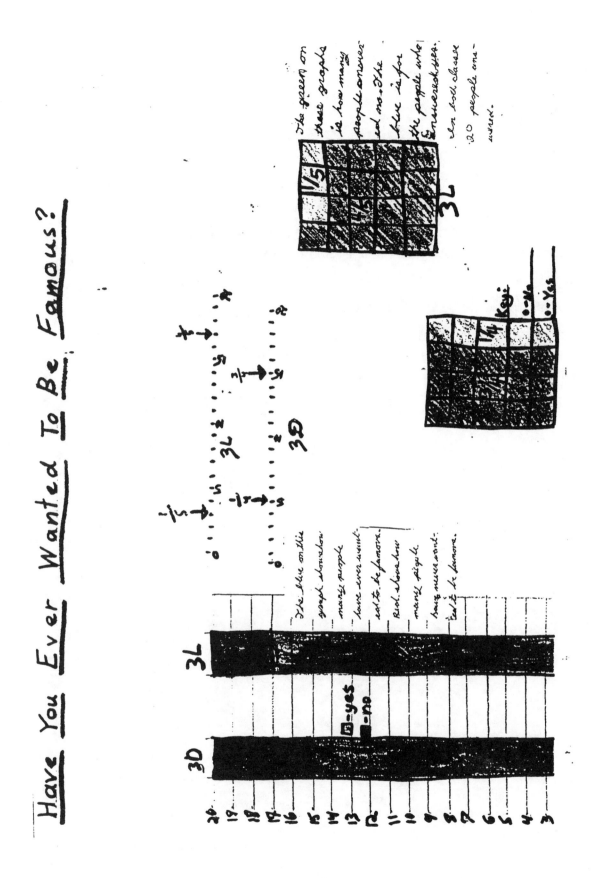

Figure 5.4

SOME POSSIBILITIES
FOR ASSESSMENT

In reporting and comparing data, students have found familiar fractions for fractions with large denominators. Sometimes the familiar fractions have been approximate; sometimes they have been exact equivalents. We suggest a question to reconsider these possibilities.

❏ Find familiar fractions for $\frac{5}{14}$, $\frac{3}{17}$, $\frac{24}{36}$, $\frac{17}{25}$, $\frac{7}{29}$, $\frac{8}{24}$, $\frac{26}{31}$, $\frac{23}{40}$, $\frac{15}{27}$, $\frac{18}{35}$ (or any fractions you choose). Students may find more than one reasonable approximation for any one of these. For example, $\frac{3}{17}$ is near $\frac{1}{5}$ or $\frac{1}{6}$, while $\frac{26}{31}$ might be approximated by either $\frac{3}{4}$ or $\frac{5}{6}$.

Some students might choose $\frac{5}{7}$ for $\frac{24}{36}$ or $\frac{1}{2}$ for $\frac{15}{27}$, while others may find the exact equivalents of $\frac{2}{3}$ and $\frac{5}{9}$, respectively. Ask students to write about their reasons for their choice or observe students as they talk about their choices in small groups.

A final word about assessment

Although ways of assessing student learning have been woven throughout this unit, you may want to find a way to look at how your class has grown and changed overall in its understanding of fractions. Asking students to describe their own knowledge about fractions can provide insight into your students' thinking. For example, you might ask students to write and illustrate or talk about their ways of answering the question, "What is a fraction?" Students could address this question both at the beginning and the end of this unit, individually, in small groups, or as a large class discussion. At first, students may define fractions in limited or vague terms, as in these responses from fifth graders:

❑   A fraction is something that is split in half.

❑   I think a fraction is defiding.

❑   A fraction is something that will tell you how much of pie you will get.

❑   A fraction is like times.

❑   A fraction is a square or circle divided perfectly in half. I'm not sure.

❑   I think a fraction is a whole something divided by a number to split it into equal sections or unequal sections.

Or, they may tell you what they think you want to hear:

❑   A fraction is fun.

❑   A fraction has two numbers, a numberator and denominator.

By the end of these sessions, you can look for evidence that students have developed a richer, more complex notion of fractions as numbers which describe many different situations.

A similar, open-ended question which elicits the depth and breadth of students' knowledge is, "Draw and write about different situations which involve the fraction 3/4 [or some other fraction]." This question works particularly well as a small group task in which different students can contribute different ideas. As you watch students work, you will be able to find out a great deal about your class's degree of comfort and flexibility in using a variety of fraction models.

Publications Available from the Department of Education

This publication is one of over 600 that are available from the California Department of Education. Some of the more recent publications or those most widely used are the following:

ISBN	Title (Date of publication)	Price
0-8011-1013-0	Adoption Recommendations of the Curriculum Development and Supplemental Materials Commission, 1991: English as a Second Language and Foreign Language (1991)	$4.50
0-8011-0883-7	The Ages of Infancy: Caring for Young, Mobile, and Older Infants (videocassette and guide) (1990)*	65.00
0-8011-0973-6	The American Indian: Yesterday, Today, and Tomorrow (1991)	5.00
0-8011-1012-2	Attendance Accounting and Reporting in California Public Schools (1991)	4.25
0-8011-0890-x	Bilingual Education Handbook: A Handbook for Designing Instruction for LEP Students (1990)	4.25
0-8011-0972-8	California Assessment Program: A Sampler of Mathematics Assessment (1991)	4.00
0-8011-0912-4	California State Plan for Carl D. Perkins Vocational and Applied Technology Education Act Funds, 1991–1994 (1991)	13.00
0-8011-0975-2	California Private School Directory, 1991-92 (1991)	14.00
0-8011-1023-8	California Public School Directory (1992)	14.00
0-8011-1017-3	California State Plan for the Child Care and Development Services Funded Under Federal Block Grant (1991)	4.75
0-8011-1036-x	California Strategic Plan for Parental Involvement in Education (1992)	5.00
0-8011-0874-8	The Changing History–Social Science Curriculum: A Booklet for Parents (1990)	5.00/10†
0-8011-0867-5	The Changing Language Arts Curriculum: A Booklet for Parents (1990)	5.00/10†
0-8011-0928-0	The Changing Language Arts Curriculum: A Booklet for Parents (Spanish Edition) (1991)	5.00/10†
0-8011-0777-6	The Changing Mathematics Curriculum: A Booklet for Parents (1989)	5.00/10†
0-8011-0891-8	The Changing Mathematics Curriculum: A Booklet for Parents (Spanish Edition) (1991)	5.00/10†
0-8011-0978-7	Course Models for the History–Social Science Framework, Grade Five—United States History and Geography: Making a New Nation (1991)	7.00
0-8011-0976-0	Economic Education Mandate: Handbook for Survival (1991)	7.00
0-8011-0856-x	English-as-a-Second-Language Handbook for Adult Education Instructors (1990)	4.50
0-8011-1046-7	English-as-a-Second-Language Model Standards for Adult Education Programs (1992)	7.00
0-8011-0041-0	English–Language Arts Framework for California Public Schools (1987)	3.75
0-8011-0927-2	English–Language Arts Model Curriculum Standards: Grades Nine Through Twelve (1991)	4.50
0-8011-1011-3	Exemplary Program Standards for Child Care Development Programs Serving Preschool and School-Age Children (1991)	3.50
0-8011-0987-6	ESEA, Chapter 2, Manual of Information (1991)	4.00
0-8011-0751-2	First Moves: Welcoming a Child to a New Caregiving Setting (videocassette and guide) (1988)*	65.00
0-8011-0839-x	Flexible, Fearful, or Feisty: The Different Temperaments of Infants and Toddlers (videocassette and guide) (1990)*	65.00
0-8011-0849-7	Food Sanitation and Safety Self-assessment Instrument for Child Care Centers (1990)	3.75
0-8011-0850-0	Food Sanitation and Safety Self-assessment Instrument for Family Day Care Homes (1990)	3.75
0-8011-0851-9	Food Sanitation and Safety Self-assessment Instrument for School Nutrition Programs (1990)	3.75
0-8011-0804-7	Foreign Language Framework for California Public Schools (1989)	5.50
0-8011-1029-7	Form J-32 State School Register, 1992 Revision (reproducible masters) (1992)	5.00
0-8011-0809-8	Getting In Tune: Creating Nurturing Relationships with Infants and Toddlers (videocassette and guide) (1990)*	65.00
0-8011-0875-6	Handbook for Contracting with Nonpublic Schools for Exceptional Individuals (1990)	8.00
0-8011-0986-8	Handbook for Teaching Korean-American Students (1991)‡	4.50
0-8011-0909-4	Handbook on California Education for Language Minority Parents—Portuguese/English Edition (1990)§	3.25
0-8011-0734-2	Here They Come: Ready or Not—Report of the School Readiness Task Force (Full Report) (1988)	4.25
0-8011-0712-1	History–Social Science Framework for California Public Schools (1988)	6.00
0-8011-0750-4	Infant/Toddler Caregiving: An Annotated Guide to Media Training Materials (1989)	8.75
0-8011-0878-0	Infant/Toddler Caregiving: A Guide to Creating Partnerships with Parents (1990)	8.25
0-8011-0880-2	Infant/Toddler Caregiving: A Guide to Language Development and Communication (1990)	8.25
0-8011-0877-2	Infant/Toddler Caregiving: A Guide to Routines (1990)	8.25
0-8011-0879-9	Infant/Toddler Caregiving: A Guide to Setting Up Environments (1990)	8.25
0-8011-0876-4	Infant/Toddler Caregiving: A Guide to Social–Emotional Growth and Socialization (1990)	8.25
0-8011-1027-0	Instructional Materials Approved for Legal Compliance (1992)	8.00
0-8011-1024-6	It's Elementary! Elementary Grades Task Force Report (1992)	5.00
0-8011-0869-1	It's Not Just Routine: Feeding, Diapering, and Napping Infants and Toddlers (videocassette and guide) (1990)*	65.00
0-8011-0892-6	Literature for History–Social Science, Kindergarten Through Grade Eight (1991)	5.25
0-8011-1039-4	Long-range Financial Planning: A Guide for School District Fiscal Policy Teams (1990)	3.50
0-8011-1033-5	Mathematics Framework for California Public Schools, 1992 Edition (1992)	5.50
0-8011-0929-9	Model Curriculum Standards, Grades Nine Through Twelve (1985)	5.50

*Videocassette also available in Chinese (Cantonese) and Spanish at the same price.

†The price for 100 booklets is $30; the price for 1,000 booklets is $230. A set of one of each of the parent booklets in English is $3.

‡Also available at the same price for students who speak Cantonese, Japanese, Pilipino, and Portuguese.

§The following editions are also available at the same price: Armenian/English, Cambodian/English, Chinese/English, Hmong/English, Japanese/English, Korean/English, Laotian/English, Pilipino/English, Samoan/English, Spanish/English, and Vietnamese/English.

ISBN	Title (Date of publication)	Price
0-8011-0968-x	Moral and Civic Education and Teaching About Religion (1991 Revised Edition)	$3.25
0-8011-0969-8	Not Schools Alone: Guidelines for Schools and Communities to Prevent the Use of Tobacco, Alcohol, and Other Drugs Among Children and Youth (1991)	3.25
0-8011-0974-4	Parent Involvement Programs in California Public Schools (1991)	6.00
0-8011-0306-1	Physical Education for Individuals with Exceptional Needs (1986)	5.25
0-8011-0845-4	Physical Education Model Curriculum Standards, Grades Nine Through Twelve (1991)	4.50
0-8011-0886-1	Program Guidelines for Individuals Who Are Deaf-Blind (1990)	6.00
0-8011-1032-7	Program Guidelines for Individuals Who Are Severely Orthopedically Impaired (1992)	6.00
0-8011-0817-9	Program Guidelines for Language, Speech, and Hearing Specialists Providing Designated Instruction and Services (1989)	6.00
0-8011-0899-3	Quality Criteria for Elementary Schools: Planning, Implementing, Self-Study, and Program Quality Review (1990)	4.50
0-8011-0906-x	Quality Criteria for High Schools: Planning, Implementing, Self-Study, and Program Quality Review(1990)	4.50
0-8011-0905-1	Quality Criteria for Middle Grades: Planning, Implementing, Self-Study, and Program Quality Review(1990)	4.50
0-8011-0815-2	A Question of Thinking: A First Look at Students' Performance on Open-ended Questions in Mathematics (1989)	6.00
0-8011-0979-5	Readings for the Christopher Columbus Quincentenary (1992)	2.75*
0-8011-0858-6	Readings for Teachers of United States History and Government (1990)	3.25
0-8011-1048-3	Read to Me: Recommended Readings for Children Ages Two Through Seven (1992)	5.50
0-8011-0831-4	Recommended Literature, Grades Nine Through Twelve (1990)	4.50
0-8011-0745-8	Recommended Readings in Literature, Kindergarten Through Grade Eight, Annotated Edition (1988)†	4.50
0-8011-0895-0	Recommended Readings in Spanish Literature: Kindergarten Through Grade Eight (1991)	3.25
0-8011-0753-9	Respectfully Yours: Magda Gerber's Approach to Professional Infant/Toddler Care (videocassette and guide) (1988)‡	65.00
0-8011-0911-6	Schools for the Twenty-first Century (1990)	3.75
0-8011-0870-5	Science Framework for California Public Schools (1990)	6.50
0-8011-1040-8	Second to None: A Vision of the New California High School (1992)	4.50
0-8011-0926-4	Seeing Fractions: A Unit for the Upper Elementary Grades (1991)	7.00
0-8011-0861-6	Self-assessment Guide for School District Fiscal Policy Teams: Budget Development, Budget Monitoring, Accounting, and Financial Reporting (1989)	3.50
0-8011-0970-1	Self-assessment Guide for School District Fiscal Policy Teams: Facilities Planning and Construction (1991)	3.50
0-8011-0860-8	Self-assessment Guide for School District Fiscal Policy Teams: Maintenance and Operations (1990)	3.50
0-8011-0857-8	Self-assessment Guide for School District Fiscal Policy Teams: Pupil Transportation Services (1990)	3.50
0-8011-0813-6	Self-assessment Guide for School District Fiscal Policy Teams: School Nutrition Program (1989)	3.50
0-8011-0980-9	Simplified Buying Guide: Child and Adult Care Food Program (1992)	8.50
0-8011-0752-0	Space to Grow: Creating a Child Care Environment for Infants and Toddlers (videocassette and guide) (1988)‡	65.00
0-8011-1014-9	Strategic Plan for Information Technology (1991)	3.50
0-8011-0855-1	Strengthening the Arts in California Schools: A Design for the Future (1990)	4.50
0-8011-0920-5	Suggested Copyright Policy and Guidelines for California's School Districts (1991)	3.00§
0-8011-0846-2	Toward a State of Esteem: The Final Report of the California Task Force to Promote Self-esteem and Personal and Social Responsibility (1990)	4.25
0-8011-0758-x	Visions for Infant/Toddler Care: Guidelines for Professional Caregiving (1989)	5.50
0-8011-0805-5	Visual and Performing Arts Framework for California Public Schools (1989)	6.00
0-8011-1016-5	With History–Social Science for All: Access for Every Student (1992)	4.25
0-8011-0989-2	Work Permit Handbook (1991)	6.00
0-8011-0887-x	Writing Assessment Handbook, Grade 8 (1990)	8.50

*Also available in quantities of 10 for $7.50 (item number 9875); 30 for $20 (9876); and 100 for $60 (9877).

†Includes *Addendum* (ISBN 0-8011-0863-2).

‡Videocassette also available in Chinese (Cantonese) and Spanish at the same price.

§Also available in quantities of 10 for $12.50 (item number 9940); 50 for $55 (9941); and 100 for $100 (9942).

Orders should be directed to:

California Department of Education
P.O. Box 271
Sacramento, CA 95812-0271

Please include the International Standard Book Number (ISBN) for each title ordered.

Remittance or purchase order must accompany order. Purchase orders without checks are accepted only from governmental agencies. Sales tax should be added to all orders from California purchasers. Stated prices, which include shipping charges to anywhere in the United States, may change after January 1, 1993.

A complete list of publications available from the Department, including apprenticeship instructional materials, may be obtained by writing to the address listed above or by calling (916) 445-1260.

R92-88 (Fifth printing) 003-0105-92 300 12-92 6,500